Follow Me

HOW TO WALK WITH JESUS EVERY DAY

Miroslav M. Kiš

REVIEW AND HERALD® PUBLISHING ASSOCIATION
HAGERSTOWN, MD 21740

The author assumes full responsibility for the accuracy of all facts and quotations as cited in this book.

Unless noted otherwise, Bible quotations are from the Revised Standard Version of the Bible, copyright © 1946, 1952, 1971, by the Division of Christian Education of the National Council of the Churches of Christ in the U.S.A. Used by permission.

Texts credited to NEB are from *The New English Bible.* © The Delegates of the Oxford University Press and the Syndics of the Cambridge University Press 1961, 1970. Reprinted by permission.

This book was
Edited by Gerald Wheeler
Copyedited by Jocelyn Fay and James Cavil
Cover design by Reger Smith
Cover photo by Corbis Images
Interior design by Toya Koch
Typeset: 12/14 Bembo

PRINTED IN U.S.A.

05 04 03 02 01   5 4 3 2 1

R&H Cataloging Service
Kiš, Miroslav Mirko, 1942–
Follow me.

    1. Jesus Christ—Teachings. 2. Christian life. I. Title.

232.9

ISBN 0-8280-1544-9

CONTENTS

To order additional copies of *Follow Me,* by Miroslav Kiš, call
1-800-765-6955.
Visit us at www.reviewandherald.com for information on other
Review and Herald products.

INTRODUCTION

"You call me Teacher and Lord; and you are right, for so I am"
(John 13:13).

Think of all the possible professions the Messiah could have chosen to accomplish His mission. Out of them Jesus selected the teaching ministry.

This book is your experience as a student of Jesus. It invites you to join His pupils, to observe Him, to feel the emotions of those around Him, and to participate in the learning events of His teaching career. Imagine yourself walking behind or alongside this incredible Master, and yes, pinch yourself occasionally, just to eliminate any doubt that *you are one of His disciples.*

In the first chapter of this volume we will examine His mode and method of teaching. Just as in a syllabus, we learn how we should behave, what to expect in the course, and what the instructor wants from us. I am happy to tell you that the most difficult and the most important requirement of this lifelong workshop is simply your *presence.*

The rest of the book follows a uniform pattern. We shadow Jesus from the manger to His resurrection. Each chapter begins with a narrative about the setting and the event. The middle section of each chapter, Lessons of Discipleship, identifies the major concepts Jesus would want us to learn from the particular event. The final section highlights the meaning of discipleship for you and me today. This application phase of learning is the most important and the most characteristic aspect of our Master's methodology. He desires to give us more than mere information. Jesus wants us to *become* like Him. Our knowledge must change who we are. *Being* is the goal of all *knowing.* And because He wishes us to *be* like Him, all of the lessons focus on Him.

Do you have a problem seeing the men and women of the Bible as normal human beings? Somehow I find myself wanting to imagine them as saints in the medieval sense of sainthood: pale and cloistered, strangers to the dilemmas and anxieties that we average people experience. For that reason I cannot identify with them easily. But in reality they are people like you and me, subject to doubt, sin, denial, and depression, but with one important characteristic: they have taken God at His word, found Him faithful, and let Him lead them through incredible adversities. This book is an attempt to paint a more realistic picture of the biblical ethos.

Additionally, because the episodes are so familiar to us, our reading and appreciation of them becomes colored too much by our knowing the ending of the account. It diminishes the impact of the story. We could compare it to knowing a punch line prior to hearing a joke. As you read these pages I hope we will be able to enter into the sandals of these everyday humans and experience the anxieties of those who did not know the end of their predicament. This kind of reading of the text may bring these brave people of the Bible closer to us, and make the application of their experiences to our situation more effective.

But remember—*no playing hooky*. When one of His disciples asked if he could bury his father first, the Professor replied: "Follow me, and leave the dead to bury their own dead" (Matt. 8:22).

Strict?

Yes.

Rigorous experience?

Yes.

A worthwhile effort?

Yes.

A reputable diploma?

Well, what does a "crown of life" look like (Rev. 2:10)? I don't know myself, but I want to follow Him and find out.

CHAPTER 1

LIFE OF DISCIPLESHIP

A military helicopter dropped us off somewhere in the forests of the northwestern Bosnian mountains. Our assignment was to patrol and return to base in 24 hours. At daylight we set out with compasses and a map. Sergeant Boris took the lead. The rest of us—Ivan, Daniel, Josip, and I—followed reluctantly.

At 2:00 p.m. Boris stopped. A sheer rock towered above us, stretching as far as we could see. Where were we? Like five tiny birds eyeing their new cage, we stood in silence. The buzz of insects and the songs of birds in the distance seemed to mock us. What now?

"Corporal Kiš." I saw Daniel and Corporal Ivan waiting. "You lead," Ivan urged.

"Lead where?"

"To the base, crazy!"

"Yeah, thanks, and where is that?"

"No one here knows where that is, but someone must take over or else . . ."

"Or else what?"

"Or else we will scatter and perish in this forgotten place. Everybody, even Sarge Boris, trusts you. That's crucial now. Get it?" By nightfall our courage had ebbed. We had no food and no clue of our whereabouts. At dawn Josip nudged me. "Sir, let me lead today. I know the way," he almost pleaded with me.

"Let you what?" bellowed Boris, overhearing. "You lead us? Never!"

"But sir, two hours from here is a waterfall. About 40 minutes southeast from there run the power lines. And two hours farther flows the Una River, the same Una that skirts our base 30 minutes downstream."

"Whew," Boris interrupted. "I didn't know you had the steam for such a speech, Josip. Kiš, let's go—you lead."

After we spent another day of stumbling around, pale and nauseated, Boris and Ivan staggered first into a small clearing. Finally we all collapsed. That night we lingered between numbness and dizziness. This could not go on, I admitted to myself. I was a corporal, but unlike Boris, my training as a medic had only the basics of orienteering. The next morning Josip finally took the lead—against Boris's wishes.

Five hours later, as we dragged ourselves through the military base gate, Boris apologized to all of us, including Josip.

"This is my country, sir. I know this land," Josip replied. Then, as if emboldened by his own humility, he added, "You were lost because you refused to follow me."

"Follow me." Consider for a moment the meaning of the words. Some kind person may give us detailed directions to help us find our way. More helpful individuals might even draw a map assuring us that we "cannot miss it." But when someone stops what they are doing and says, "Let me show you; follow me," how do you feel? After all, who has time to spare these days? Who wants to adjust their schedule, to interrupt their work, just to spend time and energy on strangers? Too few care about the acute panic of the one lost. Rare are those who so graciously identify with the plight of others that they personally guide them to safety.

When Jesus calls, "Follow Me," we hear the voice of the most gracious Being that ever lived. In His kindness He gives detailed directions for a happy and fruitful life without detours. He places in our hands an entire library of 66 books packed with invaluable help to guide us home. Moreover, He preserves for us in His Word biographies of people who have traveled the way before us, whose journeys map the safest route. But when the hills around Lake Gennesaret echoed His call, "Follow Me," that is when lost humanity witnessed the supreme display of divine grace. Jesus chose to leave eternity and enter our time. Adjusting His schedule, He left His divine rights behind and spent Himself for strangers. Zacchaeus and Levi the son of Alpheus experienced Him firsthand. It's amazing what happened.

Zacchaeus, the chief tax officer, met Jesus in a highly embarrassing position. Imagine Jesus walking down the road. Glancing up, He sees two feet dangling from a branch. Adult feet, at that! A government official stares down at Him. But Jesus does not laugh. Instead He offers Zacchaeus a new chance for change. Nothing in Christ's attitude suggests that He has an entire universe to govern, a multitude of angels to manage, numberless prayer calls to answer, the fall of sparrows to notice, and human hair to count. Jesus acts as if everybody and everything is on hold because Zacchaeus has gone astray. Zacchaeus, of course, knows little of the divine prerogatives of the Great Teacher. He recognizes only human, political, and social implications in the words of Jesus, "I must stay at your house today." *Could this be?* he wonders. *Is this some kind of metaphor, or does He actually want to eat at my table?* The man faces a momentous choice: stay on his limb, keep hiding, continue wishing for a better life while careening to his death, or come down into the open and trust the Master with his destiny. Zacchaeus chooses life—the life of discipleship. All at once he takes his mask off, revealing behind it the hideous crimes of extortion, blackmail, and coercion for his innocent victims and everybody else to see. But the terror of such consequences lasts for just a moment. For the first time since his childhood his conscience stops tormenting him. The unforgiving bureaucrat tastes forgiveness as the little man hosts the Great Master at his table. He confesses and follows (Luke 19:8, 9).

Levi, the son of Alpheus, sits stunned at his tax booth. At the words "Follow Me" his world spins. His wife, kids, house, vineyard, job security—all in exchange for trailing the new teacher? If only Jesus would have supper with his family, try to convince them or give some assurance. But no such thing happens. He, Levi, must decide, must act, and must bear responsibility for his decision. That's the kind of Master Jesus is. He is not a dictator. Christians should be the kind of people who know how to exercise their power of choice.

So Levi does the incredible, the silly, the absurd, the free thing: "He rose and followed Him" (Mark 2:14). His choice helps him understand that life through discipleship is not irresponsible, lunatic, or crazy. He need not divorce his wife, disown his children, or squander his property. Discipleship is simply a matter of priority: Jesus first. It involves investing, not divesting. "The old life is left behind and completely surrendered. The disciple is dragged out of his relative security into a life of absolute insecurity."[1] Until now Levi felt like a drunk man, holding on to things and people to keep from stumbling. But from this moment on it's like a free fall backward ("absolute insecurity" in financial terms) into the absolute security and safety of fellowship with Jesus. He perceives in that moment that Jesus is not a seller of goods or properties or an entrepreneur trading time and human resources for money. If that were the case, Levi's decision would have been sheer foolishness. Instead, he discovers that Jesus is primarily an expert in charting confused human destinies. With Him the primeval fear of the unknown loses its crippling control.

At first Levi must have felt as I did one time when plunging into a thick wall of fog at 65 mph. That evening all my adrenaline surged through my body. We could see nothing. To brake suddenly would expose us to the cars coming from behind, but to continue at the same speed could result in us colliding with oncoming traffic. The narrow shoulder gave us no alternatives. Drenched in sweat, heart racing out of control, nerves tight, and eyes peering into the white unknown, we crawled through the fog for more than an hour. Thanks to my wife, Brenda, who watched for the edge of the road through an open door, we made it to safety. But Jesus can see through even greater fog and darkness. The future is familiar to Him. He has been there. It is His country, and He knows this land. The Master does not fear decisions, because He sees the consequences in advance.

The invitation to follow evokes at least two images from the lands and times of Jesus: one pastoral, the other educational.

THE SHEPHERD

Even today shepherds in and around Israel lead their sheep by walking in front rather than behind the flock (John 10:4).

A story tells of a tourist guide who extolled the advantages of this style of shepherding. Sheep are extremely nearsighted animals, he explained, so they feel more secure when they can follow someone they trust. The voice of the shepherd gives them a sense of direction at night, when it storms, or while they graze. When the shepherds head home, they leave their flocks during the weekend in one large mass under the watch of two or three guardians. But when they return, the shepherds need only stand at the periphery of the large flock and summon their sheep. Quietly but eagerly the sheep follow the voice they know because it evokes memories of green pastures and still waters. "The reputation of the shepherd with the sheep makes all the difference," concluded the tour guide.

Suddenly, in plain sight of the tourists, there appeared a frightened flock of sheep driven from behind. The guide looked in disbelief. Incensed, he stopped the bus and in the company of the most curious passengers he began to take the unorthodox shepherd to task.

"What are you doing? What kind of shepherd are you?" he protested.

"Beg your pardon, friend," the man replied. "I am not a shepherd; I am a butcher."

Every moment of our waking hours we hear calls. They seem pleasant, compassionate, and caring. The merchants urge us to buy, the drug pushers want us to get high, entertainers sell us silly fun, and bankers claim that investment means security. But the Word of God tells us that things are not always as good as they seem at first (see chapter four). Only one among the many voices we hear is that of the Good Shepherd. The rest are butchers who need us in their own unique kinds of slaughterhouses. They delight us with their promises. "You will not die. [Lung cancer is not for you. It's for your enemies.] . . . Your eyes will be opened [so you can see for yourself; no one, no authority, will have to impose their ideas on you because] . . . you will be like God. [Now, think carefully: have you ever enjoyed such freedom? No more obedience, no more guilt; just do as you please!]" (Gen. 3:4, 5).

But once we decide to accept their offers, things change. Those charmers do not walk in front of us. They want us to face the uncertain future and the thick fog alone. All we receive are cruel blows from behind until they have securely corralled and slaughtered us.

The voice of the Shepherd is soft and unimposing. He makes no fancy promises. On the contrary, He speaks of self-denial and crosses (Matt. 10:38, 39), of persecution and poverty (Matt. 5:10-12; 8:20). But He does make and keep one particular promise: "And lo, I am with you always, to the close of the age" (Matt. 28:20). He assumes the lead if we let Him, and remains there. If we cross the desert during the day, He is the cloud that leads and shields us from the scorching sun. Or if we travel by night, He is the pillar of light shining from behind so as not to blind us (Ex. 40:38). Should we be thirsty, He is the stone from which flows the water of life (Ex. 17:6), and in the furnace of affliction, He is our companion (Dan. 3:24-27).

We do not need to experiment with Marlboros or Virginia Slims. Nicotine is a poison. Our body has no good use for it, and after a few encounters with it, it enslaves our will. Alcohol and drugs, fornication and stealing, violence and cheating, vulgarity and slander are all voices of a stranger. And because Jesus will not participate in such activities, we, His followers, flee from them (John 10:5).

The Rabbi

In the Greco-Oriental tradition, schooling did not happen inside some building full of classrooms. The teacher would have his students (disciples) follow him to the market, the fields, the garden, or the public square. There, as they accompanied him, they gleaned one morsel of wisdom after another. They learned how to handle enemies and friends by observing their teacher. His misfortune became their misfortune, his food their food, his shame their shame, and his honor their honor. Disciples took on the life of their teacher during the years of close and fruitful fellowship.

Jesus calls us to experience life as His disciples. He invites us to trace His footprints. Life is His classroom, shared experiences His lessons. Here we learn by observing His manners—gentle with those who hurt, and firm, even forceful, with those who hurt others. We have the privilege of seeing Him tired, hungry, insulted, discouraged, helpless, criticized, abandoned, and betrayed by friends, but also when He is happy, popular, successful, praised, and loved. The Master is quite willing to go with us through our daily chores. Our Saviour accompanies us to the market or the fields, the factory or the office, the garden or the public square. How fortunate to have Him walk us through our surgery or chemotherapy, through betrayal or bankruptcy. When we allow Him to share our pains and joys, to provide the necessary strength for endurance, to turn our suffering into learning experiences, He then brings meaning to even the minutest event of our daily life.

But how can we follow Jesus today? We cannot see or hear Him the way Zacchaeus and Levi did. Is this kind of talk just for mystics or visionaries? Not really. Remember when you fell in love? Do you recall how much depended on that relationship? For an entire year my fiancé, Brenda, and I endured separation. She had to complete her studies at Pacific Union College in California and I had to stay behind at Collonges, France, with my self-supporting work/study situation. More than 7,000 miles stood between us. But I lived in a different reality—the reality of her presence. Others might see little of the inner source for my dedication and energy. But inside, I felt her presence. She completely surrounded and filled my universe.

Jesus has promised His presence, but our neighbors will not see Him. They will only notice how different we are when stress or temptation taxes our commitments, how unusual our reactions and choices appear when compromises of integrity could bring us temporary advantages and success. Our neighbors will wonder where we find strength to endure and retain our faith in God and humanity in the face of war and tragedy. But Christians live in a different reality than others because the Master leads and fills their lives. Their actions and words do not reflect the stimuli, the urges, the taunting, or the insults that surround them. Christians do not react—they act. Their conduct flows from a source outside their immediate context. The long umbilical cord of faith ties them intimately to their Master, who infuses them with His style of life. Christians have a style. You can identify them by it. Their conduct is consistent and steady in the midst of changing fortunes and vacillating human loyalties and passions. Christians are like Christ, and un-Christlike people still wander alone.

COMMUNION

When Jesus asks us to come after Him, He seeks to develop a close relationship with us. He has countless lessons to teach us (John 16:12), lessons we cannot learn by ourselves, lessons relevant to our situation and our mission to humanity. And we cannot acquire such lessons only in the classroom.

First of all, God wants us to hear Jesus only. In a time when many label commitment as fanaticism, when much of the world sees truth as hypothetical and regards conviction as little more than bias, God calls for faithfulness to one Teacher. No pluralism of ideas, no indefinite open-mindedness, no relativism. Our lives must not become a consensus of all the voices around us. God wants us to distinguish between them as He did. Would we consider God narrow-minded, bigoted, or biased? Well, biased He is, for there is no other teacher under heaven who will teach us the homeward way. No other master. God wants us to carefully sort out the voices of strangers—and keep them strangers forever. When the Father says, "Listen to Him," what more do we need? Whose assessment could ever compete with His? The Father knows best indeed.

But simply observing and listening cannot accomplish our Master's mission. If we are content with hearing and watching, we cannot be considered disciples. We are merely spectators. I wonder how many churches are just sanctified bleachers for sanctified fans watching, listening, and even clapping as Jesus performs. "Every one who hears these words of mine and does not do them will be like a foolish man who built his house upon the sand" (Matt. 7:24). Such a life is just an illusory dream castle with no foundations. In calm and prosperous times, when it takes no effort to feed our families and we can walk the streets freely, a nominal, sporadic discipleship may seem sufficient. But no life, not even under prosperous Western capitalism, can shield itself from evil. When the "rains" of sickness, divorce, or death begin, or when the "storms" of war, violence, and random terrorism blow, such fictitious Christianity vanishes like the mist beneath a scorching sun. Then we act and speak and live as non-Christians, nondisciples. Even worse, we behave as nonhumans. (Need I mention Auschwitz or Bosnia?)

Jesus calls for men and women who would commune with Him. He seeks for individuals who want to share His itinerary. Some places we will go will bring us profound joy and fulfillment. We will wish to pitch our tents right there and stay on a lifelong holiday (Matt. 17:1-13). But at other times we will feel abandoned in the lonely desert or strange forest. "Butchers" will drive us from behind to places we do not wish to go (John 21:18, 19). Commitment and faithfulness to Him, to ourselves, and to humanity cannot endure unless our Christianity is a life of discipleship.

Even if we must pass through a slaughterhouse experience, we can remain confident that it is never the final destination on our Master's instructional itinerary. He is, in fact, the only Shepherd, the only Teacher who can lead human beings through the gates of death and find the exit door to resurrection. "I am the resurrection and life; he who believes in me, though he die, yet shall he live, and whoever lives and believes in me shall never die" (John 11:25, 26). The crucial question, however, lingers: "Do you believe this?" (verse 26).

So, my friends, join me in following this Master. And if we answer His call, aren't you absolutely consumed with curiosity to know where He will lead us? To see what unique experiences and particular lessons our individual personalities and temperaments need the most, in order to reach our home base next to the river of life? What decisions and partings will a life of discipleship demand? "To answer this question we shall have to go to him, for only he knows the answer. Only Jesus Christ, who bids us follow him, knows the journey's end. But we do know that it will be a road of boundless mercy. Discipleship means joy."[2] Come, let us go to Bethlehem. We will follow Him from the manger to victory.

---

[1] D. Bonhoeffer, *The Cost of Discipleship* (London: SCM Press, 1959), pp. 48, 49.

[2] *Ibid.,* p. 32.

CHAPTER 2

The Manger

PRESCRIPTION FOR PEACE

Perhaps it was a few rough boards nailed tightly together so the grain and the hay could not escape. More likely it would have been a limestone block with a cavity hollowed out to hold the animal feed. Whatever it was, we call it a manger.

Inside the stable the ever-present stench competes with the animals and the flies. And in the manger, lost in a few handfuls of hay, lies a baby. We call Him Rabboni, "my teacher." His name is Jesus.

This baby is Jesus, the Rabbi, the one who calls me to follow Him, He who has not taken even one step? Here I stand, an adult, speaking several languages, holding several degrees, with a lifetime of experience, and wonder, *Is this a joke? Can He teach me something?*

No, this is not funny! I look at that wrinkly red face, His eyes tightly shut, His toothless mouth yawning. He—my Teacher in diapers? I see this and wonder to myself, *Can this be? Can I do this? I can conceive of being Your disciple if You can present Your credentials to me or give some evidence of Your authenticity as divine Teacher. But here, in this place? If You are the Son of God, then why isn't this manger a golden crib, this stable a royal chamber, this stench orange blossom perfume, and these flies gone?*

Every Christmas the manger and stable in Bethlehem return to haunt me. And then I feel guilty. I realize that He has come. The inn has no room because I made my reservation earlier and the law protects me from eviction. The fact is that He has come too late for a room, and too early for Joseph. Joseph—that's it. He should have planned it better. If I were in charge, believe me . . .

Jesus, the Son of God, coming to our planet from heaven, should receive the best treatment that humans can give. Our hospitality must fit the worthiness of our guest. So if a person in fine clothing visits us and a poor man in shabby rags shows up, we pay attention to the one who wears designer fashions. We give him our bedroom. The poor man can go to the stable (James 2:1-4). That's just common sense, right?

But Jesus? For Him we would fancy such titles as "president," "director," "prime minister," "CEO." We would get Him a new Rolls-Royce every year (then resell it with an ad proclaiming, "Jesus used this car!"). We would give Him first-class treatment, because this is the way we reward greatness. They are our expressions of respect and love. Ours—but not God's. We value people in monetary terms. Bill Gates is worth $100 billion; a merchant next door, $2 million; and you and I . . . ?

When my sons were still small I asked them, "When you grow up, what do you want to be?"

"I will have a big house and a Mercedes, and at least two servants," one of them declared. How quickly he learned that we measure "being" by "having." The bigger, the better: bigger house, bigger car, bigger wallet, bigger plate. That's how we see things, and we are proud of it. Only great people have it big. "Bigness" is the evidence of "greatness."

And the shepherds are but one more enigma. Is it fair that they were the first to receive the news about Jesus' birth? An angel appeared *to them,* of all people! Those guys had no class, no connections, no credit cards. They certainly didn't fit in the same league with us regular people. Yet He came to them. Luke tells us: "They were filled with fear. And the angel said to them, 'Be not afraid; for behold, I bring you good news of a great joy which will come to all the people; for to you is born this day in the city of David a Savior, who is Christ the Lord. And this will be a sign for you: you will find a babe wrapped in swaddling cloths and lying in a manger'" (Luke 2:9-12).

"For to you," the angel said, "is born in the city of David a Savior" (verse 11). Do you feel the surprise, awe, and perhaps even fear the shepherds experienced? Can you imagine the strong shaft of brilliant light, the squinting eyes of shepherds accustomed to the night's darkness? Then an angel, speaking. Speaking to them! No wonder they did not know how to handle it. Never before had anyone trusted them with much of anything. Now the voice unmistakably says, "To you is born . . . Christ the Lord." Glancing around them, they saw nobody else. But what does it mean? "The Christ is given to us? A gift? Our responsibility?"

How strange! The shepherds were not the finest ambassadors of the human race. They couldn't help Joseph and Mary.

But they ran rejoicing. Singing all the way to Bethlehem. Do you know what they were singing? If they did not sing the words of Isaiah, "For to us a child is born, to us a son is given" (Isa. 9:6), then as far as I am concerned they missed the point totally.

The shepherds went with haste. We can certainly understand them. They came to see the baby Jesus—and oh, how excited they were. And how nervous and awkward. But do you think it bothered them that Jesus lay in the manger? Not at all. These people spent their entire lives in stables—with animals and stench and flies. If one of those insects would land on this baby's nose, do you think they would do something about it? Most of them had been born in a stable and would die in one. No, they showed no reluctance, no disappointment. In fact, they seemed happy that this baby came to their own habitat.

The shepherds probably burst into the stable without knocking or making an appointment. They pushed and crowded the door, stretching their necks to see, crowding close, breathing on Him without masks over their faces. Poor Mary. She had no time to rest and recuperate from her labor. Would there have been any harm in posting a sign: "VISITATION BETWEEN 1:00 AND 2:00 P.M. PLEASE—NO EXCEPTIONS!"?

We prefer the Wise Men, though. They arrived in style; well dressed and well groomed. Most of all, they came well prepared. Gold—yes, that's right on the money, Magi! Joseph, Mary, and their baby need gold so they can leave this infectious pit at once. The frankincense and myrrh could change the smell a bit around here, but the market price of such commodities suggests a better use of them for this poor family.

If we have a choice, we would rather have money, gifts, reputation, and class to offer as a gesture of support. Then we can head back to our businesses in haste. To study with this baby as professor? We would rather decline for now, thank you.

LESSONS OF DISCIPLESHIP

But Jesus? He stays here, lying in the manger, in the stench of His stable, pleading with us to stay a while. The infant professor's lectures begin here and now. Jesus in the manger teaches several lessons.

1. LESSON OF TRUST

The baby Jesus sleeping quietly in His manger demonstrates first the lesson of trust. He shows that human life is happy and useful if it is sheltered by Someone who will not betray us. So He chooses to begin His teaching ministry as a baby. Never is a human being more vulnerable and helpless than during the first days and months following birth. Nowhere could Jesus be as exposed and susceptible to harm as in the stable. In no situation could the salvation of humanity teeter more precariously than in the manger. But this is God's work—God's errand that Jesus is on. His plan and honor are at stake. Jesus comes empty-handed, weak, and naked so we can be assured that no tricks lingered somewhere up His sleeve. Empty-handed, He can teach us how to trust in His Father's riches. Weak, He can make God's power more evident during times of danger. Naked, He can show how God protects, nurtures, and cares for our daily needs. His Father is worthy of our trust. We too can take Him at His word and follow Him with confidence.

Jesus in the manger illustrates that discipleship is not a commercial venture. Prudence in business requires that our investments be safe, that the decisions of our broker be astute, and ultimately that sufficient profit fills our bank account. We sign contracts and engage insurance policies to shield us from unfortunate losses. But when Jesus calls "Follow Me" and then stoops down into the stable, He promises nothing more than the complete trustworthiness of His Father's guiding hand. "If any man would come after me, let him deny himself and take up his cross and follow me" (Matt. 16:24). Jesus is not a business partner, nor is heaven a financial institution. A life of discipleship in exchange for material profit regularly fails, as Judas could tell us. The rewards of discipleship are richer and incomparably more valuable than anything money can buy.

2. Lesson of the Supreme Value

When Jesus bids us follow Him into the manger, He urges us to alter our value system drastically. Our treasure, our highest priority, determines where our heart will be (Matt. 6:21). He calls us away from the biggest and most prestigious things of this world to instead cherish the things of the spirit, mind, and character. "For what will it profit a man, if he gains the whole world and forfeits his life?" (Matt. 6:26). "Seek first his kingdom and his righteousness, and all these things shall be yours as well" (Matt. 6:33). Here is His order of priority. Yes, our daily bread, clothing, and wallets are important to us. But when our self-image depends on such things, when our sense of security rests on possessions, then we have not yet learned the wonderfully liberating lessons of the manger. We may still be under the tyranny of "having" at the expense of "being."

3. Lesson of Gratitude

When Jesus invites us to follow Him into the manger, He teaches us the lesson of gratitude. Left to ourselves, we will never be satisfied, never content with what we are or what we have. It is not without reason that at least two commandments of the Decalogue directly prohibit envy and covetousness. From His manger Jesus reminds us, "When you have a roof over your head, a simple bed to lie upon, sufficient food to nourish your family, and an abundance of love to warm your home, then you have reached My standard of life. It might not fit the U.S. standard. But it *is* My measure of well-being."

John, a close neighbor of ours, acquired a little fortune during the destitute years after World War II. His sheep yielded a rich crop of wool. Surprised and elated, John, a new Seventh-day Adventist

Christian, made a quick plan. "I will go to the fair next month," he confided to my mother, "and I will buy the best pair of horses available on the market and a new horse cart. And Nataly, instead of going home directly, I'll go through all the streets of the village with my prancing horses and brand-new cart so the world can see how God blesses the converted Christian."

"I'll pray for you, John," is all my mother said.

A few weeks later, the evening of the fair, my mother heard John's voice calling her. Mustering all of her energies, my mother came out ready to face his pride and joy.

"John! John, but what . . . what is this, John?"

"Yes, Nataly, this is all I need for now," came the enigmatic reply.

"But these ponies will never grow. They are only a bit bigger than your shepherd dogs! What can you do with these tiny horses?"

"Nataly, these ponies will do just fine."

"What do you mean, John? These beasts cannot pull a plow! What will you do? Did Melanie see this?"

"No, my wife did not see them yet. But I wonder if you could go and prepare her for the shock. You see, Nataly, when I arrived at the fair and checked out the horses . . ."

"You did not have enough money." My mother supplied the difficult words.

"No, I had plenty of money. But I felt strange. Something began to grow in me. Just to be among those rich people made me feel so special, so good, so superior. Pride, Nataly. I must call it pride. So I wondered, *John, do you need pride? No,* I replied to myself. *Well, then, you do not need these beautiful horses.* What I needed were these ponies. Nataly, I went from the best, most expensive horses, down the price range. Only with these ponies did I not feel better than average. Please, go and speak with Melanie. Tell her I need just these ponies. That *I* need them!"

4. Lesson of Human Worth

Jesus in the manger teaches us that we cannot express the worth of a human being in terms of any known value. We may need to appraise someone's assets, behavior, skills, or habits in order to relate to them properly. Perhaps we may prefer one person above another for many reasons. But humanness belongs to a different sphere of reality than behavior, skills, habits, and assets. Such criteria have no power to express human worth. A physician has irreplaceable skills for a medical emergency we may face. Her help is of exceptional value to us. It could make a difference between life and death. But that says little about the physician as a person, nor can it reveal her worth as a human being. Her weight, height, origin, status, age, or gender has no significance in assuring or establishing her humanness. No, Bill Gates is not worth $100 billion, nor are you worth 100 cents. In fact, as human beings, Bill and you are of equal importance and worth. All humans are "created equal." The American Constitution has it right. Creation, that's where it all began, and that's where it all remains—in the hands of the Creator. Nothing and nobody can take it away unless we choose to neglect it. Our worth proceeds from, resides with, and remains in Him. Real human value is unfathomable, and we cannot, and must not, even try to express it in such terms. We have no currency to assess it in. The whole world sinks into insignificance in comparison with the value of a human soul (see *Counsels to Writers and Editors,* p. 126; *Testimonies for the Church,* vol. 5, p. 624). Only Calvary reveals its worth through the price paid for our ransom (see *Gospel Workers,* p. 184; *Testimonies for the Church,* vol. 3, p. 188).

The Baby in the manger, what is His worth? What price tag can we attach to Him?

All our Rolls-Royces parked in front of that stable, all our Rolexes, titles, and medals would fade into shame in the presence of the genuineness, simplicity, and plain humanness of the Baby. Shepherds, unlike us, felt comfortable in that stable. They were happy to see Him there because He became *their* Lamb. The Lamb and the shepherds had nothing to give, nothing to boast about, nothing to hide behind—not even proper manners. They had nothing to give but themselves. The shepherds came just as they were, exposed and real, to see the Baby, just as He was, exposed and real. And God wanted it so. The royal chamber, the golden crib, the orange blossom perfume, and the absence of flies would disguise Christ's real humanity that He came to incarnate. Such titles as president, director, prime minister, or CEO would intimidate the very people whom He sought to draw to Himself. Titles and commodities tend to mask and overwhelm our sense of humanness, too.

So the true greatness of the Magi resides in their genuine human simplicity in spite of their wealth. No one, not even the king, could intimidate them into a conspiracy against the Baby in the manger. They were able to bend low and render homage to Him in the company of the animals, the stench, and the flies. But they would not bend their principle of loyalty even at the risk of their lives. No, bigger is not greater. The smallest among us demonstrates his greatness by daring to be seen and treated as the smallest in his own eyes and in the eyes of others, too.

MEANING OF DISCIPLESHIP

A stable and a manger—what a setting, what lessons! It's all so strange for those of us who own a house, a bed, a car, perfumes, and aftershave lotions—who see those things as absolute necessities for a normal life.

So what are we to do now? Are we to sell everything, buy a stable somewhere at the edge of a village, prepare a manger, and sleep in it just as the Master did?

No, not yet. One day it might come to that. Hundreds and thousands experience just such a tragedy during war. The soldiers force you to sign over your entire property to someone you never met, someone you may never see, without even a thank-you in exchange. An entire life's labor, sweat, and savings forever gone. The next minute you stand alone on the street. Everything remains behind with just a dark oppressive fog ahead of you. You linger in absolute disbelief . . . cold heavy stones filling your gut. But the soldiers push you to move on with nothing in your hands: no wallet, no picture albums, no perfume.

During such calamities the true disciple of the Master really stands out. If our heart identifies with His kingdom, not with our possessions; if our self-respect does not depend on titles and human recognitions, then our security is indeed in a secure place. In situations in which thousands lose their sanity, health, or even life, the disciple keeps on—because from the stable and the manger the call of the Master sounds: "Follow Me."

No, Jesus does not expect us to lodge in stables in the company of animals, nor to sleep in a manger as a proof of our discipleship. The lesson of the stable and manger means something entirely different. First, it signifies that as followers of the Master from the manger in Bethlehem, we place His kingdom and His righteousness at the top of our system of values. With this value as our dominant criterion, all our desires, pleasures, dreams, hopes, and all other goals recede to their rightful place. No more do we find ourselves driven to compete with our neighbors for first place—for the bigger, more extravagant thing. We are ready to sell everything. Ready because things do not dominate our life. And we are able to give up the position of repute in exchange for divine treasure, because, unlike many, we recognize the enormous value of His kingship in our lives (Matt. 13:44-46). Even if the Master does not ask us to sacrifice everything, we are still prepared to do so. There is no better, no more secure investment than eternal values with eternal earnings. No rust, no thieves, no soldiers can ever separate us from this wealth, this kind of freedom.

Second, the lifestyle of the stable and manger considers persons above possessions and being over having. Beautiful prancing horses at the price of genuineness and simplicity of human heart is never a deal worth making. Neglect of a spouse or children for the sake of vocation or achievement, be it even a church-related career, does not harmonize with the steps Jesus would take. "We have often suffered from degradation by poverty," argues Abraham Joshua Heschel. "Now we are threatened with degradation through power. There is happiness in the love of labor, there is misery in the love of gain. Many hearts and pitchers are broken at the fountain of profit. Selling himself into slavery to things, man becomes a utensil that is broken at the fountain."[*]

Third, if we decide to become His disciples, we cannot expect material gains. The Person we follow, the lifestyle we adopt, the nature of the people we become, and the kind of destiny we choose greatly outweigh any material concerns. Who we are is much more important than what we have. "Indeed I count everything as loss because of the surpassing worth of knowing Christ Jesus my Lord. For his sake I have suffered the loss of all things, and count them as refuse, in order that I may gain Christ" (Phil. 3:8). Our hearts are alone satisfied and our desires quieted in His presence. A house is a bonus, the car a gift, the wallet a tip, the bed a present, and the screens on the windows to keep the flies out—that's gratuity. Anything above the Jesus standard is a blessing and a privilege. Our eyes are not oriented toward more and always more, but rather back to the manger where Jesus sleeps. No matter how poor or wealthy we are, our sense of security, our feelings of worth, derive from whom we know, whom we follow. It comes from an attitude of unquenchable gratitude: a perspective, a lifestyle, that would not intimidate the Baby in the manger or His friends the shepherds. We feel good only when Christ can feel at home in our house. When hearts overflow with gratitude, a stable looks like a royal chamber, the manger appears as a golden crib, the stench smells as orange blossoms, and the flies do not matter, because our heart is simply a roughly made manger in which Jesus rests peacefully.

------

* Abraham Joshua Heschel, *The Sabbath* (New York: Farrar, Straus and Giroux, 1951), p. 3.

CHAPTER 3

The River

AT THE CROSSROADS OF DESTINY

For several months my enthusiasm for my work faded away. On the surface, nothing had changed. Plenty of customers and exceptionally good income would normally make me thankful and happy. But deep down in my heart I knew that repairing watches and clocks as a lifelong vocation was not for me. But who could understand? My frustrations only increased when my mother heard about it. "How can this be, son? Just a little more than a year ago you started with no capital. Now, at the age of 22, you bought a house for cash, your business is growing, and your income is greater than I have ever experienced since your father died. Can this be anything less than a miracle? Can you toss away such a divine blessing—just like that?"

Well, the fact is that I did not deal with the issue lightly. I understood my mother's feelings. A devout Seventh-day Adventist Christian, she was committed to the church. But to see her son go to school now! Letting go of financial security, so reminiscent of the time before my father was killed 20 years before, became a serious subject of discussion. My sister said nothing. Yet, frankly, I suffered more from seeing her reaction than from anything she ever said. Her face reflected a strange mixture of anxiety and resignation.

We were used to such reversals of fortune, except that until now we had been the innocent victims of tragic events. I remember daydreaming about staying on for the sake of my mother and younger sister. How happy we all could be. So for three additional years my business flourished. But I knew that the restlessness, the urge, the call to leave everything and join the Master in His work, would not cease until I answered it.

In the humble carpenter shop at the edge of Nazareth similar thoughts raced through Jesus' mind. From the moment the news of cousin John's preaching at the river Jordan reached town, Jesus' work, which had provided both means and meaning, now lost its appeal. The bench, the tools that Jesus knew so well, every nail in the wall and every crack in the floor, felt more and more distant. So one day Jesus swept the floor, arranged the tools, hung up His apron, and placed the "Closed" sign for the last time. He left all in response to the call from His Father. The next day He began the 64-mile-long journey from Nazareth to the place called Bethany, on the banks of the river near Jericho (John 1:28, 29).

As John the Baptist glanced over his listeners that day, his eyes caught sight of Jesus. He had seen many people lately. John remembered the hard, stony face of a cruel criminal melting into the face of a repentant boy. A shrewd merchant had squinted carefully around him in search of his debtors. A drunkard, crushed under the weight of his addiction, had mumbled words of praise for his newfound freedom. The Baptist thought of the faces of multitudes who had come to him bearing heavy loads of guilt. Many of them, both rich and poor, erudite and illiterate, Jew and Gentile, soldier and civilian, had, under the conviction of the Holy Spirit, experienced the incredible power of grace. They came to him hopeless and helpless, and left the waters of baptism with joy and peace in their hearts.

John knew those faces. He had learned to read them as open books. But in this face he sensed something unique, something fresh and genuine. The pure innocence of a child wore the mature and robust face of a man. Ellen White comments: "Among the multitudes that had gathered about him at the Jordan, John had heard dark tales of crime, and had met souls bowed down with the burden of myriad sins; but never had he come in contact with a human being from whom there breathed an influence so divine." [1]

To say the least, Jesus was different. His work, His insistence on honest dealings, could pass in the provincial town of Galilee, but not here. These people came from Jerusalem and other adjoining towns where life was a little more sophisticated. The customer could not trust the merchant, the citizen was suspicious of the civil servant, and even the so-called nobility—the ruling caste, the king on his throne, and the priest in the Temple—lived in corruption and selfish indulgence.

You see, everybody does it. *This is normal.* Standards of right and wrong do exist, of course, *but we live in a sinful world* (the seven last words of all integrity). Do unto others before they do it unto you is the only realistic gospel of the street, of business, of politics, of the committees that constantly shape our lives.

So spoke and thought and acted the people who flocked to John. And a good thing they came. At least some of them sensed how far society had gone and how close to disaster it stood. The Scripture account notes that multitudes flocked from Jerusalem, Judea, and all the region around the Jordan, and being baptized by John, confessed their sins (Matt. 3:5, 6). "What shall we then do?" they pleaded (Luke 3:10). The majority, however, ignored John. They accepted the law of the jungle and learned how to cope and profit.

So, yes, Jesus did not fit. He had no skills to outsmart, outwit, or manipulate His way through the "real world." Nor did He resort to lies as a means to produce good, to cheating for gain, to compromise when justice hung in the balance. Mary and Joseph had not raised Him streetwise. They had directed His mind toward wisdom from above—wisdom that "is first pure, then peaceable, gentle, open to reason, full of mercy and good fruits, without uncertainty or insincerity" (James 3:17).

In this crowd Jesus looked like a lamb among the wolves, and John did not hide his surprise to see Him. Had He come on a business or sightseeing trip, had He come to visit His cousin and relatives, or had He decided to pass by on His way to Jerusalem at the onset of His ministry, John would have understood. But to come sinless and request baptism for the forgiveness of sins—that made no sense at all. "I need to be baptized by you, and do you come to me?" John protested (Matt. 3:14).

But Jesus did not flinch. "Let it be so now," He urged, "for thus it is fitting for us to fulfil all righteousness" (verse 15). All righteousness, John—all. "I have come this far, and I'll go all the way for sinners." So John consented. "And when Jesus was baptized, he went up immediately from the water, and behold, the heavens were opened and he saw the Spirit of God descending like a dove, and alighting on him; and lo, a voice from heaven, saying, 'This is my beloved Son, with whom I am well pleased' " (verses 16, 17).

LESSONS OF DISCIPLESHIP

So, my friends, here we are at the banks of the river Jordan. A beautiful place to be. Listen now. Jesus' words and actions teach us important lessons of life.

1. HUMAN SOLIDARITY

As I listen and watch Jesus mingle with people, His behavior confuses me. He is different, but not indifferent. Although He doesn't fit, yet He enjoys being here. His eyes carefully avoid suggestive looks, but He is not a hermit or a monk avoiding contact with sinners. While He is visibly disturbed when He hears rude, filthy words, He still claims this crowd for His own.

"What is this, Master?" I feel like telling Him. "Why are You confusing us? Why don't You act like Your cousin John? At least he is consistent. He dresses strangely, lives in the desert, eats odd food, and keeps a safe distance from people. If they come to him, it's because he's so different from everything they know, and that makes his message ring true. Aren't You afraid of confusing Your followers? You have come to the river, but You dress normally, You eat and drink and visit with people, yet right here in front of them You act differently. Your company doesn't match Your ways. Master, I see two risks. First, I'm afraid many will turn away, scandalized by the company You keep (Matt. 9:10, 11). And second, Your company may reject You because You do not fit in. People can handle only so many sore thumbs, you know."

Fortunately, instead of teaching, I settle for learning. Jesus' behavior models how to be an agent of change for good without letting the evils around us transform us instead. The key word is solidarity. Solidarity with people. Jesus focuses His attention and His care on human beings *before* He reacts to their ways. He studies and identifies with their needs *before* responding to them and *before* dismantling their strange and harmful coping mechanisms. The Master does not begin with seeing them as drunkards or criminals. Rather, He first regards them as people who resort to drinking, who develop addictions, who act violently, and in the process hurt themselves as well as others. Every sincere suffering soul feels secure in His presence. They have assurance that He understands them. And as they become acquainted with Him, they observe how He copes with some of the same issues of life with which they struggle.

The crowd at the Jordan attracted His attention as a sick, suffering child tugs at a physician's heart (verses 12, 13). He came as Messiah, as Saviour, and saviors always rush to the victim's side. The Master is here *because those who need Him are here.* Jesus came to the Jordan River out of solidarity with His kin. His compassion overcame embarrassment, and His power to help transcended all fear.

2. LESSON OF TIMING

When Jesus requested baptism from John He taught us to follow God's leading at every stage of our lives. "Let it be so now," He counseled. Until yesterday His Father had kept Him in the carpenter shop, and tomorrow He may open new horizons and duties. But now is neither yesterday nor tomorrow. Now is a time with its own demands and opportunities.

A disciple learns that the Master chooses both the itinerary and the pace. Disciples follow, not lead. They cannot run ahead and still follow. Nor can they insist on taking another route if the Master did not pass that way. Jeremiah knew that "the way of man is not in himself, that it is not in man who walks to direct his steps" (Jer. 10:23). "The way of a fool is right in his own eyes, but a wise man listens to advice," concludes Solomon (Prov. 12:15). At times the pace will slow down to a halt. Then *following means waiting.* Moses experienced a miraculous rescue from certain death when Providence intervened on his behalf at the river Nile. It was clear evidence of God's planning and leading. And yet for 40 years he followed by waiting and seemingly wasting his skills and schooling on a herd of sheep. Yet it can give us a sense of security to remember that God's purposes know no haste and no delay.

3. THE THREE MOVEMENTS

The baptism narrative depicts the downward path that Jesus takes as He descends into the river. God incarnate, the sinless Son of man, teaches us that all important beginnings start with modesty. Humility is the crucial virtue of human character. With wonder we watch Jesus assume His place in God's plans. He who holds the universe in His hands abandons Himself into the hands of His creature to be lowered below the surface of the water where human beings cannot survive. For a few extraordinary seconds John holds the real Master of the universe in his grip, his mind dizzy, his muscles quivering under the weight of responsibility. For an incredible and powerful moment Jesus lies there in the water, His self-defenses down, ready to serve the needs of others at His Father's bidding.

Then comes the second movement, one that goes upward. His leg and arm muscles bulging, John watches the water slowly part to let the peaceful face of Jesus reappear. Jesus looks up. Up is where the path of duty calls. From this place in the river, the spot where He identified Himself with sinners and was identified as their Substitute (John 1:29), the path will lead Him upward until Roman soldiers lift Him up on the cross. And then He will draw all humanity to Him. But now, at this juncture in time, He must climb the steep road bearing the heavy burden of loneliness, misunderstanding, and conflict. Some will love Him intensely, and others will bitterly oppose Him. His closest friends will never be close enough, nor friends enough, to minister to His great needs. He will have to blaze the trail alone, a daunting task that could frighten anyone. How can God place such an impossible assignment on the shoulders of any human being?

The answer came quickly. "And when Jesus was baptized, he went up immediately from the water, and behold, the heavens were opened and he saw the Spirit of God descending like a dove, and alighting on him" (Matt. 3:16). His amazing self-resignation (the movement down) prepared Him for His impossible mission (the movement up), which triggered an instantaneous descent of the Holy Spirit (the movement down) to empower Him and render the impossible task a possibility. We see all of this before our eyes and wish so much that our Master's experience would become ours.

4. LESSON IN INNOCENCE

As we see Jesus in the crowd at the river Jordan we wonder how He feels. In some ways the experience must seem to Him like being a foreigner in a strange land, speaking a different language and think-ing differently. Yet His strangeness does not result from cultural or linguistic differences. Jesus is in His native land, and Aramaic is His native tongue. Moreover, He socializes well. People come to Him easily. He understands, and cares for them. It is more His innocence, almost naïveté. He could not engage people on the latest scandal in Washington, D.C., nor discuss the hot news about some Hollywood escapade. It is more the kind of innocence one may expect of younger people. Jesus blushes, visibly uncomfortable with off-color or indecent remarks. The man looks immature and inexperienced in sinful sophistication. And so He was.

Most certainly He remembered the words of Isaiah the prophet—terrifying words for someone who actually needs to iden-tify with them. "He had no form or comeliness that we should look at him, and no beauty that we should desire him." Try to live one week as "despised," "rejected," "one from whom men hide their faces." Or see how you would cope with the consequences of "we esteemed him not," "we esteemed him stricken, smitten by God, and afflicted" (Isa. 53:2-4). Here at the river He began to sense the full force of that kind of status: an innocent servant in the midst of fallen and debased friends.

At times He must have wondered about His role and work. He must have been tempted to allow Himself a compromise or two, just so He could fit in for a moment. Just so He could approach people more closely, make His lessons more vivid, win people for God's king-dom. It would have been compromise for the sake of evangelism.

I praise God that He resisted such temptation. We have a Master who was tempted in all points, but who gained victory every time. He teaches us that inexperience and innocence with sin are OK. The culture around us might not be too impressed, but the Master knows best. For His disciples, His assessment counts more than other people's opinions. No one can achieve integrity through compromise.

5. Lessons in Lofty Revenge and Lowly Reverence

As we follow Jesus to the river, we meet John the Baptist. What a man! Jesus would say of him, "I tell you, among those born of women none is greater than John" (Luke 7:28). He can teach us a unique lesson in Christian living. John Calvin articulates his admiration of the Baptist in these words:

"Think of the majesty of this John. Remember how he bore himself in the presence of the Pharisees and Sadducees; and how he faced Herod, telling him plainly, at the risk of his life, as it afterward proved: 'It is not lawful for thee to have thy brother's wife.' Remember that all Judea, and Jerusalem, and Galilee had been bowing down in his presence. And now, when an obscure, nameless One of Nazareth comes to him, only as yet distinguished from others by the holiness of His life and the purity of His soul, John would not have Him bow in his presence, but would himself bend low before Him. 'I have need . . .' Oh for more of that grand combination of lofty courage and lowly reverence."[2]

6. Lesson of Commitment

But why does Jesus need John to baptize Him at all? It cannot be for forgiveness of sins. Jesus' explanation to John, "Thus it is fitting for us to fulfil all righteousness," seems to indicate a twofold sense of duty by which He felt bound. In the first place, it involved Jesus' commitment to His Father, and second, it arose from His commitment to save fallen humanity.

Now, at the beginning of His public ministry, Jesus sets the tone and marks the parameters of what He will do. His Father is at the center, and His will is sovereign. Even if it does not make sense to human reason, Jesus still proceeds with baptism in following God's prompting. Though He is sinless now, He still is on the territory of the enemy. Like everybody else, He will be tired, tempted, stressed, hurt deeply, deserted, and lonely—circumstances that will put His resolve and single-mindedness to the test. His baptism signaled a public statement, a covenant, a promise to give priority to His Father's plans.

Moreover, Jesus as the Messiah represents the repentant Israel who came to the river to be baptized for the forgiveness of sins.[3] His mission requires Him to identify Himself fully with the penitent people of God in order to be their Saviour.[4] A time will arrive when His family and closest disciples will try to dissuade Him from carrying through with His task. But His promise at the river, sealed by the anointing of the Spirit, will remain unmoved until its full realization.

MEANING OF DISCIPLESHIP

How can we live the lessons learned at the river Jordan today, in our time and culture?

First, in His prayer Jesus identifies His followers as men and women who are in the world and yet not of the world (John 17:14-17). *He* places us here. We belong to our communities, but we do not blend and vanish into them. Our ways are often radically different from those of our neighbors and friends, but we are equally as human as they. As we look around us we notice those who emphasize their presence through boisterous behavior, rich apparel, or lofty titles. Apparently they have a need to stand out, to make a statement, to affirm their status. I once addressed a former student of mine as "Mister" during a meeting. Afterward his wife remonstrated forcefully because I did not use his title of "Doctor." Our natural impulse is to assert ourselves or to correct others. To let them know that such behavior looks petty and repugnant. But then we remember Jesus. It's amazing to see how invulnerable and secure one feels when liberated from the spirit of rivalry.

Rough and profane words foul the air around us. We detect their speakers' satisfaction as they invent some caustic joke at the expense of someone's position, race, gender, or nationality. They try to affirm themselves or infect others with their own anger. Or frightened, they attempt to scare or impress others. Reacting swiftly, our tongues sharp, we instantly want to respond. But we remember Jesus and His contrast. He gives us the power to remain dignified and calm. Only then can we minister to those who offend us. Disciples of Jesus stand out because they are different. Others blend into the surrounding culture because they all have the same need to be noticed.

Yet because of Jesus we insist on staying here, befriending people and caring for them. We choose to belong here where we cannot blend in, because we want to help insecure, emotionally disturbed, and evil-addicted humanity. But we do not do it out of pride or condescension, because we remember our own history before we came to the river. Compassion leads us on.

Ivan, a friend of mine, got caught in Sarajevo during the atrocious war of the nineties. Because of his involvement with ADRA International, he could go in and out of the city. For years he and his coworkers were the only mail service allowed across the lines of demarcation between all three fighting armies in Bosnia. Often the military officers treated him with a special respect.

"Why don't you just split?" they would ask. "No one forces you to do this. You're taking your life in your hands whenever you cross the lines."

"I am under orders too, you know," he would reply calmly. "I must do this. Jesus would have done it."

People such as Ivan draw others like a magnet. They are honest and unpretentious. In their company the ostentatious spontaneously try to hide their own gaudy facades as they see the inner charm shine through others. *How can this be?* they wonder. *How can anyone so modest and humble be so confident? How can they command respect and convince others without swearing and intimidation?*

When Jesus calls us to follow Him into the crowd at the river, He implies that we should reach out to the secular, befriend the worldly, belong with them without blending with their ways. He longs for us to come closer to them and win their trust so they can catch a glimpse of Him through our lives. As they see our common needs and frailty they will no doubt wonder at our source of strength, peace, and resourcefulness. It might be that some will want a taste of our faith, a portion of our sense of purpose, and ultimately they might wish to join us in following our Master.

Second, in the light of our experience at the river, we see that God is interested in every detail, every moment of our lives. How much more pleasant and acceptable in the sight of His family and friends would Christ's life have been if He had stayed in the carpenter's shop. But nothing, not even the ultimate sacrifice, could divert His course from His Father's plan. No matter what our job or what our calling may be, Jesus urges us to press closer to Him, to follow His leading. If we lag too far behind, we may lose sight of Him and miss our way. Just one moment of distraction could be harmful. In my experience, that meant leaving my watchmaking business in order to follow Jesus in pastoral and teaching ministry. But I know watchmakers who did not receive such a call, who remained at their posts, and at the same time remained very intimate with the Master. It could be that some of them may be closer to Him than I am in spite of my present calling. A life of discipleship knows no caste, no privileged class. Here at the river we are all sinners. We are all lost in the forest, searching for our way back to the base. But we have found the only One who is not lost.

Third, we are challenged to step down to the level of a pupil. Pride born of self-centeredness, or fear of humiliation and failure, keeps many from becoming disciples of Christ. But no one needs to feel humiliated by Jesus. He is the most gentle and understanding teacher you'll ever meet. During my teenage years I wondered why God created us inferior to Himself and then required us to worship, adore, bow down, and pray to Him. Was He some kind of a self-serving God? Later, in college, I realized that we never serve Him first— He washes our feet before we get the idea. We never pray first—He stands and knocks, and His promptings remind us to pray.

Once we come down to His level and He begins to lead, the only way we can go is up. Up to accept our life calling, up to confront the forces opposing life and goodness, up to take a stand on the side of the unfortunate and marginalized just as He did. And whenever human beings begin an impossible task for God, He cannot remain at a distance and watch. He comes down and energizes and blesses our efforts. His Spirit opens our eyes to new methods. God leads us to the right people and gives us the right words to say.

Fourth, just as in the time of John the Baptist, our generation needs disciples who have courage and reverence rightly focused. Courage to swim against the current, to uphold truth and acknowledge falsehood. Like John, such men and women will not hesitate because of the risk to their own position or approval rating. But at the same time they are people who will humbly listen to the Master's advice and follow Him as a trusting lamb does the shepherd. That also is a life of discipleship.

Finally, Jesus calls us to bind our destinies with Him. Promising to stay with us until we are safe, He will complete His work of redemption in us (Phil. 1:6). That is His commitment. Will we pledge our faithfulness to Him, though? His perfect life, His death, and His resurrection will amount to nothing for us unless we vow our exclusive faithfulness to Him. Remember, many other guides also promise unbelievable happiness if we follow them. Family, friends—all of society may entice us to join them in pleasure seeking. And unless we are bound to Jesus with unbreakable ties, committed to go only where He would go, we will put our destiny in danger.

A young friend of mine came with his younger sister to her Bible study as she prepared for baptism. He appeared concerned that his sister was still young, being only 14 years of age. Should she make her commitment to Jesus now? "Pastor," he pleaded with me, "I was baptized at the same age. But later, when I wanted to enjoy life with my friends, I could not, because I remembered my promise at baptism."

"What kind of enjoyment, Peter?" I asked.

"Well, the kind you would call sinful."

"And what would *you* call such enjoyment?"

"I know, Pastor, but I did not feel free to do what I wanted."

"Who stopped you?"

"My promise. I'd given my word."

"Well," his sister chimed in mischievously, "I am *very* glad you made your decision early, my boy! I want to be baptized now!"

Today, at the river, we meet Jesus at a turning point of His life. Every human being encounters such days. In the morning things look normal. We remember our plans, our unfinished tasks, and we think we know the schedule. Instead, before the day is over, our life has permanently changed. Without knowing it, we have reached the crossroad of destiny. A phone call, a letter, an e-mail message, and from the quiet regularity of a little town we find ourselves thrust into the uncertainty of an itinerant lifestyle. Or instead of the bonds of a small family, our task now embraces solidarity with the entire human race. No more socializing only with a select like-minded few. The Holy Spirit propels Jesus' followers into a mixed crowd in which even dangerous characters feel at home. There, in the muck of society, God calls us to blossom into lilies. Our commitment, our roots, reach into secret depths where the clean source of life-giving waters spring forth.

---

[1] Ellen G. White, *The Desire of Ages* (Mountain View, Calif.: Pacific Press Pub. Assn., 1940), p. 110.

[2] John M. Gibson, *The Gospel of St. Matthew, The Expositor's Bible,* ed. W. Robertson Nicoll (New York: A. C. Armstrong and Son, 1908), vol. 15, p. 33.

[3] Donald A. Hagner, *Matthew 1-13, Word Biblical Commentary,* ed. David A. Hubbard and Glenn W. Barker (Dallas: Word Books, 1993), vol. 33A, pp. 56, 57.

[4] R. T. France, *The Gospel According to Matthew, The Tyndale New Testament Commentaries* (Leicester, Eng.: Inter-Varsity Press, 1985), pp. 94, 95.

CHAPTER 4

The Wilderness

FACE-TO-FACE WITH THE LION

We had no proper fishing gear, so we improvised by twisting an ordinary needle into a fishing hook. Through its eye we thrust a string and tied it securely, slipped on a bottle cork, and attached the other end of the string to a long stick. No such things as sinker, reel, or lure existed in our world. With an ample supply of earthworms, we went fishing. It was the destitute, starving years after World War II, when everyone spent their time gathering food. To our amazement, the invention worked well. Fish could see only a harmless string and a hopeless worm. Not knowing that the string was attached to it, they sampled the bait . . . and the hook, too.

Today the fish have even less of a chance. The perfectly transparent nylon line vanishes in the water. With a variety of baits, sinkers, and lures, fishers easily deceive their prey. There they stand on the shore in the cold morning, just when the fish are ready for breakfast, and "generously" hand out the food. Wonderful!

But the truth is tragically different. *Things are not the way they appear.* Hooks hide inside some of life's tasty morsels. Strings are attached to them.

That's how we humans treat other creatures. We catch the fish, trap the foxes, trick and deceive both birds and animals. We are superior to them. The fish cannot hook us; the foxes will not trap us; the deer cannot hunt us; and the elephants will not take advantage of us.

Human beings hold dominion, and they don't. We can fish just for fun, wounding their jaws just for sport. All because we are able to hide the hook, conceal the trap, and camouflage our presence and intentions. Animals must endure our abuse and oppression because they cannot return the favor or sue us for harassment, bodily harm, or intentional death.

As for us, we walk our planet with the conviction that we are secure, lucky, and untouchable. But God has sent us word that *things are not as harmless as they look*. Behind the innocent landscape of the familiar, the very air we breathe is deceiving. A ferocious "roaring lion" is on the loose, stalking us every minute "seeking someone to devour" (1 Peter 5:8). His particular delicacies are those who have been to the river and pledged their allegiance to the Master. Those who have decided to embrace a life of discipleship.

Jesus experienced His face-to-face confrontation with the lion right after His visit to the Jordan. The Bible is not particularly eloquent about it. A simple "then" moves us from a wonderful experience of divine affirmation of our Teacher to a troublesome statement: "Then Jesus was led up by the Spirit into the wilderness to be tempted by the devil" (Matt. 4:1).

From the lush greenery of the riverbanks He quite literally went up, most likely into the range of Mount Nebo from where Moses, centuries ago, looked over the Promised Land. Its landscape earns the name "wilderness" even today.[1] But the contrast is not as troublesome as the assertion that the *Spirit* led Him into a deserted place so the devil could tempt Him. Why would the Holy Spirit play such a role? It almost looks as if God waited for a high moment in Jesus' experience in order to deliver a low blow.

We must examine this and related questions later. They hold invaluable lessons for us. For the moment let's focus on the Master. Scripture says that Jesus prayed and fasted 40 days and 40 nights. Matthew adds an obvious fact: "Afterward he was hungry" (Matt. 4:2). But in that very situation, at the moment of vulnerability, the devil intervenes with a most relevant suggestion: "Jesus, you're hungry. Eat! Eat, man!" "Eating is one of the three highest goals of the human life," says a Slovenian proverb. "What the other two are has not yet been discovered."

How nice of the devil. How caring! Who said he is our enemy? Jesus has been so absorbed in prayer and communion with His Father that He might have overlooked food and other legitimate needs. Clearly His Father did not think to feed Him. Perhaps Jesus forgot the divine power He possessed to take care of His physical needs. A little prodding—a hint—and Jesus can feed Himself.

To that the Master simply quotes the Scripture: "It is written, 'Man shall not live by bread alone' "(Matt. 4:4, quoting Deut. 8:3). That is to say, "It is not relevant what I need. Nor are my feelings normative. The desire of my physical nature is not life's highest value. I am more than an eating machine." God created human beings for nobler purposes. We see their true and full dignity evidenced when they live "by every word that proceeds from the mouth of God" *(ibid.)*.

The devil does not reply, and a fearful scowl crosses his face. Have you noticed that he does not argue with God's word? Instead, he shifts away from the subject. Having observed with horror what the word of God can do during the six excruciating days of Creation, he is terrified at its power to transform, to create new things and new people. And because Satan does not want to expose himself to the influence of God's word, he changes the subject.

But notice how he does it. "Then the devil took him to the holy city, and set him on the pinnacle of the temple, and said to him, 'If you are the Son of God, throw yourself down; for it is written, "He will give angels charge of you," and "on their hands they will bear you up, lest you strike your foot against a stone" ' " (verses 5, 6; Satan quotes Ps. 91:11, 12).

Remember how it all began? First the Spirit took Jesus into the wilderness. Now the devil has an almost free hand with Him. From first being alone with God, He must suddenly be alone with the enemy. The Spirit watches without interfering.

The devil is a master at using the element of surprise. He removes Jesus from the solitude, the silence, the place where winds and thoughts share the freedom to go where they will, and plunges Him into the noise of a bustling city. The Master finds Himself standing on the vertiginous height of the Temple.

"Wonderful!" the devil says. "You did not want to use Your divine power for Yourself. Great! But to inaugurate Your ministry in style, to catch the public's attention, Jesus, why don't You jump without a parachute? Humans know the power of gravity. Imagine! You jump—they see You. They shriek and close their eyes to avoid seeing the horrible splatter. Instead, You walk among them. No broken bones, not a scratch! Right here You can start a tremendous campaign, preaching Your kingdom.

"Besides, You know, this is not entirely my idea. You seem to know Your Bible. So do I. I just quoted from the Scriptures, so it must be OK. All You would do is demonstrate that God really means what He says in His Word."

Picture yourself in Jesus' place. You look down as people stop to watch. They point with their fingers in your direction. Excitement builds up. A master of showmanship, the devil makes it appear that jumping is a matter of faith for Jesus.

But is it? Jesus checks His memory just to make sure Satan did not misquote Scripture. No, he has cited the verses by heart, word for word.

Quickly, as Jesus searches His mind, He remembers that He has never understood Psalm 91 this way. The devil tries to stay faithful to the text, but how can he arrive at such a conclusion? He is a master at twisting meanings. So Jesus quickly examines Satan's interpretation. If He jumps, what would the reason be? Human actions based on divine promises must not be motivated by a desire to test God or to impress the crowds. Otherwise God would be busy all the time responding to His children's whims. So Jesus replies to misapplied Scripture: "Again it is written, 'You shall not tempt the Lord your God'" (Matt. 4:7, citing Deut. 6:16). Jesus knew His Bible well, aware not only what it said but even more important, what it meant.

Again no reply. It is frustrating when you assume that people genuinely want to converse with you, to share with you their views, but when challenged, they switch subjects and never resolve the issue at hand. So the devil remained quiet. Instead he "took him to a very high mountain and showed him all the kingdoms of the world and the glory of them, and he said to him, 'All these I will give you, if you will fall down and worship me'" (Matt. 4:8, 9).

Satan did not use Scripture this time. Too much of a risk. Since he cannot trick Jesus on biblical grounds, the devil resorts to the ultimate temptation, the most potent agent of corruption: *power.* Since it had perverted him, the mightiest angel, it just might derail Jesus, too. Imagine the impact his offer of being king of the whole earth could have on the human Jesus!

But, of course, it would not come without strings attached. "If you will fall down and worship me, Your Father will understand. You are a human being now. Besides, You do not even need to mean it. It's just form, You know. Policy. That's how it is here on earth. When in Rome . . ." "To you I will give all this authority and their glory; for it has been delivered to me, and I give it to whom I will. If you, then, will worship me, it shall all be yours" (Luke 4:6, 7).

But Jesus will not lean on any prerogative, any skill, any power—only the authority of God's Word. "Begone, Satan! for it is written, 'You shall worship the Lord your God and him only shall you serve'" (Matt. 4:10). No pleading, no requests, just a direct, unambiguous command: "Begone!"

Finally Luke informs us that "when the devil had ended every temptation, he departed from him until an opportune time" (Luke 4:13).

LESSONS OF DISCIPLESHIP

If you ever follow Jesus into the wilderness, I can assure you of one thing: you will never forget the experience. No one could ever encapsulate all the impressions or learn all the lessons from an encounter with the devil in action.

1. UNRELIABLE REALITY

The first impression that grips the Master's disciple in the wilderness is an overwhelming sense of insecurity. There is actually no place where we can be safe. To go to the desert, away from the cities and their enticements; to seek to flee people and stress; to spend time in fasting, prayer, and total devotion to God—none of these can protect us from the most powerful criminal at large. No desert is so remote, no place on earth so holy, no mountain so high that it can hide us from the demonic lion. The world has no place or time that can ensure complete peace. When, after he tried "every temptation" on Jesus, the devil vanished—but he departed only for a time, simply waiting for a more opportune moment.

2. Values as Baits

Have you seen them, the larger-than-life posters? A strong, young, healthy, charming, vigorous man on a splendid horse with gorgeous clear mountaintops in the background. On the bottom of the placard the big bold letters spell "Marlboro." Is it bait? Does it have a hook inside? a string attached? You better believe it *before you bite!* At first glance you see nothing evil except a cigarette between the man's fingers. But you get the message loud and clear: "Smoke! You do want to be as handsome, as strong, as healthy as this man, don't you? So smoke. That's cool, man! We care about you; about what your friends think of you. You'll have plenty of fresh crisp mountain air between the puffs. Plenty of healthy lungs in you. Don't act so old and stuffy!"

Most of the values around us can be baits. The devil is not stupid. He knows we prefer value to duties. So he camouflages sin under the garb of a value, something desirable. Hides it under something precious or attractive. If he would tell the truth, he would picture at least one of those models emaciated, dying on their hospital bed with tubes and IVs, desperately struggling for the next breath. Marlboro and emphysema, tobacco and lung cancer fit together as cause and effect. Cigarettes mean sickness and death for smokers as well as those trapped with them in the same bedroom, the same home, or the same office, bus, or park bench.

But the devil is not stupid! To tell us the truth about drugs, movies, dancing, heavy rock, the occult, alcohol, or cigarettes would be like fishing with a naked hook or trapping with no bait. If you hear people exclaim, "But I see nothing bad about it," believe them. The fish do not see it either. The devil does his job well. All we see is a value. The consequences? Who cares. We ignore them for the sake of immediate pleasure.

Values are powerful motivators, but also potent baits. No one can make a safe decision if the only concern is value. Nor is anyone secure who bases his or her decisions on appearance. *Values are not as special as they seem. Sinful creatures in a sin-infested world need help to see through values, to check for hooks.*

3. NEEDS AS BAITS

Everyone has needs. The concept enjoys an enormous respect in modern civilization. It explains, excuses, and justifies almost anything.

I am stressed; therefore, I *need* to reduce my internal tension. So I shout, abuse, and hurt others.

I am depressed, so I *need* a drink or dope.

I am young and beautiful, so why not satisfy my *need* for adventure, love, and pleasure?

I am poor, and a little stealing from the rich will satisfy my *need*.

Tony Walter articulates how needs often control marital relationships as well: " 'I love you, darling' has become 'I need you, baby.' Marriage today is not the mutual giving of self, but the mutual meeting of each partner's needs by the other; if one partner's needs are no longer being met by the other, then this is widely deemed as grounds for divorce. 'I could no longer meet his/her needs'; 'he/she could no longer meet my needs' is the cry of the partner who walks out, and this is accepted in many circles."[2]

But needs, whether genuine or false, easily become a tool in the devil's hands. Notice how he waited 40 days and nights while Jesus fasted. At that point food was what Jesus needed the most. The big liar comes to offer himself as a savior of the Saviour. Bread, the most basic element of food, is right at hand. No one would blame Him for satisfying such an essential need. But you cannot trust the devil—not even when he tries to help. He never misses a chance to stuff his "acts of benevolence" with hooks.

4. USING GOD

I used to think that teacher's pets were the most despicable creatures on earth. After 17 years of teaching I can recognize them almost immediately. Rather than despising them, I now feel sorry for them. Terrified of failure *and* of hard work, craving prestige but also inherently lazy, they try to achieve without effort. We can find them everywhere, not just in the classroom. Whenever the powerful, the rich, or the famous give them special consideration without justifiable reason, when they single them out above others, when to them the rules do not apply, teacher's pets thrive.

Being a special child, student, or employee can be a very perilous privilege—perilous to both pets and teachers. In place of hard work or rigorous study, a new habit appears: the fine art of polishing apples until they shine. Generosity, empathy, and kindness can be addictive on the receiving end. The Bible notices how "the poor is disliked even by his neighbor, but the rich has many friends" (Prov. 14:20). More riches, more power, yield more pets. More pets, however, yield less respect and more potential for abuse of the teacher's kindness.

The devil recognized the power of this human weakness. He also knew that Jesus was very special—*the unique Son*. He heard it from God's very mouth, "This is my beloved Son" (Matt. 3:17), and he could not bear the thought. Since the creation of our world he had felt discriminated against. Satan assumed that Jesus was spoiled—spoiled to the point of abusing His Father's promise of protection. Whatever Jesus would ask, His Father would give Him.

And as we watch the struggle atop the Temple, as Jesus resists the urge to plead special consideration, we learn the lesson of true discipleship. Yes, Jesus is the unique Son of God, but even He cannot—and would not—behave as a teacher's pet. "Although he was a Son, he learned obedience through what he suffered" (Heb. 5:8). He sought no special treatment for Himself, or special exemptions for His disciples, either. His path is not the direction of least resistance, but the way of courage and single-minded endurance in faith.

5. POWER AS BAIT

Within the span of a few short days a friend of mine (we'll call him Sam) moved from the position of simple foreman to an executive post of power. He recalls how it felt when people suddenly noticed him, greeted him, and sought his opinion and attention. Almost overnight his word became law. Awareness of his new power transformed his feelings toward his enemies, his friends, and himself. A new sense of extensive freedom opened an unbelievable range of possibilities. He could do whatever he wanted. The buck stopped with him.

Then one day Sam found himself asked to resign. He had no choice, really. When we talked, it became clear to both of us what had happened. Very gradually Sam began seeing himself not as Sam, but more and more as vice president. He thought of *himself* as powerful, free, and important. As a vice president he grew larger than life in his own eyes. He forgot that it is the position that gave him his new prerogatives, that when he became vice president nothing changed inside himself.

The day the real Sam, the Sam of foreman days, died, he became the most impotent person in that company—and he did not know it. Because he neglected to nurture himself, he became vulnerable to bribes, compromises, and abuses of power.

The devil knew long before anyone coined the saying that power corrupts, and that absolute power corrupts absolutely. That is why he reserved the ultimate power bait as the last temptation. But again he was gravely mistaken. The Master did not aspire to power. He refused to identify with the political hyenas of His day. As we observe and admire Him in silence, Jesus, the man, is just that—Jesus the man. Just as He did not require a golden crib and orange blossom perfume before He would enter this earth, so now He fits just fine in His human skin. We learn that office, title, status, or any position of power is not fundamental to humanness. Such things do not belong to our essential nature. We put them on either as responsibilities or as barnacles; either as Saul's armor or as five smooth stones in David's pouch. But the winner is neither the armor nor the stones. The winner is the character of the man and woman making their choice to be true to the Word of God.

MEANING OF DISCIPLESHIP

While visiting my relatives in eastern Slavonia (Croatia) we came close to the border. No one could move unless a soldier-guide walked in the lead. He gave one single instruction: "Follow me." The soldier carried a mine detector, and bright-orange rope bordered the narrow path. Suspended on the rope hung bilingual Croatian/ English signs: "Danger—Mines." Carefully we obeyed our leader and the warnings to the letter of the law. No one felt guilty of legalism here.

As we walked, I looked around at the familiar landscape. The trees, the grass, the song of the birds—everything looked so normal, so harmless, so innocent. A beautiful butterfly landed, then fluttered around, mindless of the guide and the signs. For a moment I felt like the little boy who used to run around these meadows catching this butterfly's ancestors. But now I had to stay on the path. *Things are not as innocent as they look.*

Jesus says, "Follow Me. Eat and drink what I would eat and drink. Go places I would visit, and avoid those places I would shun. The world is rigged with 'mines,' all custom-made. They are meant for you, and only My way is safe."

So what does the victory of Jesus in the wilderness mean for us today? How can He help us? What are we to do? First, the episode in the wilderness makes it very clear that there is no true Christianity other than discipleship. A Christian follows the Teacher not because of curiosity or an insatiable thirst for knowledge, but out of life-and-death necessity. The intensity of our commitment and closeness to the Master is directly proportional to our awareness of the viciousness of sin. Its ever-present threat is a reality. Therefore it would be foolhardy to venture alone even for a moment.

Second, the whole experience in the wilderness says to us today that values are treacherous. You cannot trust them implicitly. The best mask for evil is good. Why is it that filmmakers mingle the pure with the impure, the noble with the base, and the refined with the vulgar? Music makers do the same. They know that the *Christian crumbs* will attract the Christian youth to an *unchristian banquet*. The devil knows that Christ's disciples still struggle with fatal attractions. He also recognizes that these weak points can serve him well as welcome mats. Additionally, he has skill at placing the good stuff at strategic places. Satan positions a few Christian crumbs to whet a Christian's appetite, and then he serves a banquet of filth.

This leads us to a very sobering conclusion: *a disciple of Christ rejects decisively any obvious evil, but approaches an apparently good thing— a value—cautiously. When on the enemy's ground God's followers will regard goodness as suspect until proven innocent.* Only on the narrow path with Jesus' footprints in it can we be safe. I often hear people say "I see nothing bad with dancing" or "What's wrong with jewelry?" Every time I both concur and cringe. Of course we cannot see! The devil is not stupid. He knows how to hide his bait. *But why do we feel a need to pay him a compliment?* He does his job well anyway!

Third, Jesus' experience in the wilderness demonstrates that a life focused on needs can be extremely vulnerable to temptation. Anything that we obsess over or concentrate on can throw our entire sense of priorities out of balance. The very intensity of our craving attracts Satan's attention as an antelope does a hungry lion. It is all he waits for. If you hunger for amusement, he will give it to you. Whether it be pleasure, recognition, power, or money, he will provide it, but in a way that will make you desire more and more until you forget the weightier matters of life. Self-gratification and the avoidance of discomfort at any price soon dominate the heart, the mind, and all our energies. We begin to ignore our character, our friends, even our health, diet, and sleep. Satan has trapped, hooked, or snared us when we let needs control our lives.

A disciple shall not live for needs alone, but for the Master alone, and then—only then—will all true needs be fully met as well.

Fourth, a life of discipleship is one of watchfulness. "Watch and pray that you may not enter into temptation," Jesus cautions (Matt. 26:41). Is He asking me to be careful? to examine my every step? I can watch as much as I want and still risk my life. Impossible! This discipleship business may be too stressful for me.

And it would be if we do not let Jesus accompany us. "Watch with me," He urges His disciples (verse 38). We do not have to walk across the minefield by ourselves.

We are not alone on our journey, just as He did not want to be alone in Gethsemane. Because He also watches, because He can see farther, and because He loves us too much not to help us, we can be safe. Besides, since the devil suffered the final defeat on Calvary, he cannot ever again tempt Jesus. In fact, he dare not even come near Jesus. In this way, as long as we keep close to the Master, the devil will keep his distance from us because he fears Jesus, and we can enjoy our rest.

But there is more—much more.

I remember the feelings that precipitated my decision to stop fishing once the food shortage subsided. The sport did not excite me anymore, because it was an unfair game. We had a most definite advantage over the fish. So I dreamed about helping the fish defend themselves. Perhaps if I could learn the fish language I could whisper a warning to them. I would summon them away from the place where the fishers "generously fed" them.

Unfortunately, my thought remained just an idea. The fish are as defenseless now as they were then. But we humans need not be in a similar position. Jesus can speak to us today. He can warn and advise us. Through His Holy Spirit He has access to our minds, so we can count on hearing the Word behind us saying, "This is the way, walk in it." And what is even more assuring is the fact that He will speak to us right at the moment of decision. We will hear it just at the place where the way branches to the left or to the right (Isa. 30:21).

When my mother convinced me that the fish had no language, my imagination raced even faster. What if we could invent fish glasses? The kind that would help them see through the bait. So as they swam along and saw some morsels of food, the glasses would reveal which bit was bait and which one was safe to eat.

Again, the fish are out of luck and we humans are blessed. There do exist "glasses" that can enable us to see through the devil's trickery. Jesus Himself used them during each of Satan's assaults in the wilderness. We have the Bible. It is the written record of dangerous places, of harmful companions, of injurious food and drinks, and of poisonous influences and actions.

Unfortunately, the Word of God is useless unless we read and study its messages. Jesus knew His Bible. He knew it so well that His Father's will became His own. The Father's outlook became His worldview, the Father's preferences His own choices, the Father's vocabulary His speech, the Father's goals His ambitions, the Father's dreams His passion, and the Father's plans His life story. At the end of the 40 days Jesus was ready. Not because He was Jesus, but because He knew the Bible and committed His life to its instructions. And in the whirlwind of temptation, when He needed it the most, the stories, the historical events, the commandments and counsels, as well as the promises, all came to His mind so clearly that He could detect Satan's misinterpretations and misuse of Scripture. In that traumatic instant the knowledge of His Father's Word assisted Jesus to perceive the path to follow.

That was Jesus. But can I do the same thing? My work requires me to read student papers, some newspapers, and many books and other materials. I must meet people, sit on committees, cultivate friendships, travel in airplanes, and most of all, provide for, enjoy, and love my family.

And so did Jesus. All of it—except for airplanes. But He traveled, not as far nor as fast, but certainly as long, much less comfortably, and in much more exhausting ways. He knew the traditions of the fathers, kept up with the news (He heard about the fall of the tower of Siloam), and He led a fruitful social life. His family, it is true, He left behind when His public ministry began. But then He adopted a "family" of 12 adult, rugged, very different men. Try that for three and a half years. In addition, He had women and others who accompanied Him on His travels.

Vulgarity, quarrels, violence, and promiscuity assaulted His ears and His sight. While He was sensitive to human suffering around Him, and while He hurt when people caused pain, the idea of imitating an evil act or harboring a malicious thought remained off limits. His mind functioned on another wavelength—not because He was Jesus, but because of the Bible. The Bible assimilated into the very cells of our being helps us discern between values and baits, between opportunities and temptations, and between true and false needs. Following Him, we can walk with our head high, our life secure. The old devil will catch nothing today. He will have to open a can of sardines instead.

---

[1] *The Seventh-day Adventist Bible Commentary* (Washington, D.C.: Review and Herald Pub. Assn., 1980), vol. 5, p. 309.

[2] Tony Walter, *Need, the New Religion* (Downers Grove, Ill.: InterVarsity Press, 1985), pp. 2, 3.

CHAPTER 5

MEETING THE PROTOTYPE

He had no training as a watchmaker, but he fixed watches well. People liked his low prices. Despite the fact that he had no sophisticated tools, he could handle almost anything. For his equipment or part needs he depended on us, because we had a license that gave us access to supply stores. As far as I was concerned, the man was a very nice, unobtrusive, polite nuisance.

My boss and master, Mr. Hacko, treated Mr. Koolich with collegial respect. They would joke, talk serious business, share knowledge freely. Mr. Hacko told him stuff about watches he had not yet told me, his apprentice. *How strange!* I thought. Finally one day I asked why we gave this man supplies at wholesale price and why we encouraged and supported our own competition. We could easily and quickly stop him, especially since I had to deal with some mistakes he had made when his clients would later bring their watches to us for correction.

My master listened to my youthful reasoning, and said quietly: "Miroslav, remember, competition is always in your head. Even when people do try to compare themselves to you, you must not allow the spirit of competition to ruin your dignity and respect. Do you feel threatened? Mr. Koolich has problems with his eyes, so he could not become a professional watchmaker. We can help him. He does not try to beat us, but is a friend in need."

We are in Jerusalem. The Master has arrived for the annual Passover festivity. After the supper Jesus steps out for a walk and His evening meditation. I imagine Him approaching a garden and, sensing that uneasy feeling of being followed, glancing behind Him but seeing no one. Farther down on the path Jesus finds a low-bending olive tree, a comfortable place to sit and review the events of the day. Then He hears it again, the footsteps on the path and the clearing of someone's throat. A figure, dressed in rabbinic regalia, approaches. *H'mmm,* Jesus might have thought. *This is unusual. Who do you think this is? And why here? Why now?*

As for the visitor, he has wanted to see Jesus for some time now, but under two conditions only: First, he insists on a one-on-one meeting. Second, the meeting must remain an absolute secret. Jerusalem is his nation's political, cultural, and religious center. To be a leader of a synagogue in another town—that's an important position to be sure. But to be a Pharisee and "a ruler of the Jews" (John 3:1) in Jerusalem—that's of a different league altogether. Such a responsibility has its limitations and restraints. Caution is of the essence.

Nicodemus's visit comes at a time when Jesus enjoys great popularity. John 2:23-25 tells us of the incredible attention His activities received. People from all over came for Passover in Jerusalem, and He healed them, spoke to them, and won their sympathies and support. "Many believed on his name when they saw the signs which he did" (verse 23).

Finding a place to sit down, Nicodemus begins to speak. His voice rings true and friendly. His compliments and courtesy come from a sincere heart, and Jesus decides to converse with the refined scholar. Nicodemus chooses his words carefully. "Rabbi," he says, "we know that you are a teacher come from God; for no one can do these signs that you do, unless God is with him" (John 3:2).

Imagine how you would feel hearing a similar statement from such an important person. "Rabbi." With one masterfully chosen word Nicodemus declares his acceptance of Jesus among the great masters of his time. A leader of the Jews in Jerusalem calls Jesus "my teacher." What he says next is even more surprising. Nicodemus is not alone in thinking this way. He seems to speak for his fellow

Pharisees when he continues, "We know that you are a teacher come from God." Jesus did not seek or crave official recognition, and yet this visit, and what the night visitor declares, confirms the fact that His ministry has had an impact on the powerful party of the Pharisees. Observing Him carefully, they have concluded that "no one can do these signs . . . unless God is with him" (verse 2). The tone of conversation now set, Jesus can speak as a legitimate fellow rabbi.

And so He does. "Jesus answered him, 'Truly, truly, I say to you, unless one is born anew, he cannot see the kingdom of God' " (verse 3). No "Thank you, Nicodemus, for your kind words," no transitional sentence. Instead Jesus directs the conversation in a definite direction: the kingdom of God. The reason Jesus had been born, it was the overarching motivation for all His activities.

The abrupt shift must have surprised, if not slightly displeased, Nicodemus. He had probably come with a different agenda. John the Baptist had already identified Jesus as the Lamb of God and left a strong hint that He was the Messiah. If that was the case, and Jesus made such a strong showing among the people, then should not Nicodemus and his fellow Pharisees do something about securing their proper place in the coming Messianic reign? The momentum was building, and they had no time to waste.

Jesus knows all of this. He can sense His growing popularity, but He is not too impressed with His fans. "Jesus did not trust himself to them," and for a good reason: "because he knew all men and needed no one to bear witness of man; for he himself knew what was in man" (John 2:24, 25). Jesus understands Nicodemus's thinking on the subject, and instead of reacting to the words of His visitor, He addresses the man's thoughts. Their conversation appears disjointed only on the surface. Both know very well what is going on.

Except that Nicodemus does not immediately capitulate. He asks a rhetorical question: "How can a man be born when he is old? Can he enter a second time into his mother's womb and be born?" (John 3:4). We all know none of us have any second chance. Ah, if I could be born the second time, and at birth have all the experiences I have now, wouldn't that be nice? In theory we can imagine anything, but life is not speculation. We—the grown-up people who are already born—want to see the kingdom of God take place now, in our time. What can we say about that possibility?

Jesus' reply repeats a more elaborate and specific version of His previous statement: "Truly, truly, I say to you, unless one is born of water and the Spirit, he cannot enter the kingdom of God. That which is born of the flesh is flesh, and that which is born of the Spirit is spirit. Do not marvel that I said to you, 'You must be born anew.' The wind blows where it wills, and you hear the sound of it, but you do not know whence it comes or whither it goes; so it is with everyone who is born of the Spirit" (verses 5-8).

In His first statement Jesus tells Nicodemus that *no one* can *see* the kingdom of God (verse 3). Now in His second statement He tries to explain to His friend that new birth prepares a person for *entering* the kingdom (verse 5). By verse 7 Jesus becomes even more straightforward. He switches from the impersonal third-person "one" to the direct second person plural: "Do not marvel that I said to you, '*You* must be born anew.'"

The second chance, the possibility to have a new beginning, is not some fantastic dream. And no, it does not happen through the mediation of a person's mother's womb. This time the birthing occurs through the working of the Spirit within a human being, and that is out of human control. The Spirit, like the wind, has His own purposes, methods, and tasks, and all we can observe is the results.

At this point Nicodemus finds himself lost. He has received much more than he expected. So much for his own agenda! Jesus opens to him mysteries he never studied in rabbinical schools. Fascinated and intrigued, he drops all defenses and admits his bewilderment. "How can this be?" It is all too fantastic and mysterious, and yet it touches the very destiny of human life.

His hunger for knowledge wins, however, and Jesus responds in kind. For the final stretch of the conversation Jesus retains His position of a teacher while Nicodemus becomes a disciple. "Are you a teacher of Israel, and yet you do not understand this? Truly, truly, I say to you, we speak of what we know, and bear witness to what we have seen; but you do not receive our testimony. If I have told you earthly things and you do not believe, how can you believe if I tell you heavenly things? No one has ascended into heaven but he who descended from heaven, the Son of man. And as Moses lifted up the serpent in the wilderness, so must the Son of man be lifted up, that whoever believe in him may have eternal life" (verses 10-15).

A sharp, scalpel-like cut opens the true condition of this venerable man. He listens to Jesus, but his mind has been working on a different plane, an earthly one. But like a pupil holding an exam paper Nicodemus has to face the moment of truth. In the classroom, with his students, he might conceal his ignorance in a variety of ways. Here, however, is someone much younger than he, but Someone who knows the human heart, and Nicodemus also recognizes that his "grade" is not very impressive. Nicodemus has taught about God, about salvation, about the kingdom of God, and about eternal life, but as theories and traditions. Theological phraseology proves dismally inadequate when we actually face God, salvation, the kingdom, and eternal life. Both of them are teachers, but while one is an objective searcher for truth, the Other is Truth Himself. Nicodemus is a theologian, and Jesus is Theos.

LESSONS OF DISCIPLESHIP

This episode reminds me of my college years at Collonges, France. One day a delegation of scholars and officials from the ecumenical movement came to our campus to become better acquainted with Seventh-day Adventist theological positions. What we experienced then, those of us who had been lucky enough to stay on campus that summer, surpassed all our imagination. We saw for the first time our professors dialogue with their peers, articulating their Christian faith and hope in ways they never could do in the classroom. To us it was a real discovery. To convince us, their students who had come to learn—to answer our questions—seemed an easy assignment. But to see other scholars ponder and reflect on the wonderful themes of the Bible and then leave impressed—that affected us profoundly.

I wonder what people would have thought if Jesus had avoided dialoguing with the intelligentsia of His time. How would His disciples through all the ages have felt had He associated only with those who thought like Him—if He preached and fellowshipped with His fans only? But Jesus was the Master. He could face anybody, and the truth that He incarnates will change lives permanently. We see it happen this evening with Nicodemus, and then with us.

1. LESSON OF INTELLECTUAL HONESTY

As we contemplate Nicodemus, his dignified stride, his aristocratic manners, and his reputation, it amazes us that he would take this unusual step and seek out Jesus. Only a short time earlier Jesus had taken off His carpenter apron, while Nicodemus's career spanned longer than His entire life. As a leader of the most elite and most powerful segment of society, he could have refused offhandedly any new ideas, any new teachings. Many in his position and at his age become consumed with defending the old ways. He was in the time of life when one could enjoy the fruits of one's labors and receive recognitions, medallions, and doctorates *honoris causa*. It was time to pass on his wealth of knowledge to younger generations. But Nicodemus struggles with some issues, and he cannot and will not pretend that everything is all right.

He and his friends wonder about the soon-coming Messiah. They are aware of what the Magi knew about Daniel's prophecies, and Nicodemus looks for hints as to where Jesus sees Himself in the scope of things. Is He the Messiah? As we watch Nicodemus sit and absorb Jesus' condensed, tight reasoning about the new birth, we learn an important truth: no one, no matter how erudite, intelligent, or powerful, ever graduates in the school of Jesus. We detect no pride in Nicodemus's reactions, no debative spirit, no fault-finding scrutiny, and no criticism.

A true disciple never need feel humiliated to learn something new, but discipleship does require humility. Without it no one can learn anything. Commitment to our Master and His teachings and a firm resolve to remain unyielding in defense of truth does not mean a stubborn refusal to hear and examine any deeper probings into that truth. Openness is not tantamount to doubt or compromise. But it does mean a readiness to grow continually. "Morning by morning he wakens, he wakens my ear to hear as those who are taught" (Isa. 50:4). A disciple is more eager to learn than to teach.

2. LESSON OF INTELLECTUAL PRUDENCE

Nicodemus has his ideas about Jesus. The more he watches Him, the more it seems that the future of his nation—and indeed of the world—depends on this Rabbi come from God. In some ways he reminds me of Judas, yet in other aspects he is a very different person.

Judas dreams similar dreams about the Master. The longer he associates with Him, observes His moves and actions, the more he too becomes convinced that Jesus must be the Messiah his people have been waiting for so long. Surprisingly enough, this very conviction leads him to betray his Master. But whereas Judas acts treacherously, Nicodemus, in the same situation, with similar convictions, steps forward to defend his Master (John 7:50, 51; 19:39). What a contrast! How is it that while Judas spends years with Jesus and Nicodemus sees Him only occasionally, still Judas is a traitor while Nicodemus remains a trusted and risk-taking friend?

The crucial difference lies in the fact that Judas never finds the time, or desire, to sit down with Jesus, to lower his defenses, to allow Him to get close. Judas never opens his eyes wide enough so that he can see the entire panorama of future events. Jesus' betrayer never allows Jesus to spell out for him His own mission. He keeps his gaze too narrow to see the Saviour's real purpose on earth. On occasion Judas might have felt tempted to abandon the Master, because He did not fit his idea of the Messiah. At other times, though, Judas felt convinced that Jesus was the one he looked for and used his influence to impose on the other disciples his restricted point of view. One wonders how much Judas contributed to the doubt, the competition, and the rivalry among the other 11 disciples. Did he delay their awareness of the spiritual foundation for the work of salvation?

Not so with Nicodemus. Before he would start to act, speak, and plan for the coming reign of the Messiah, he first decided to go to the King Himself. His wisdom had taught him that his ideas could be totally off base, and that Jesus must build His kingdom from the foundation up. David could not fight Goliath in Saul's armor, and the kingdom of God must not be imposed on the Messiah by His subjects.

The privilege of discipleship demands our openness to Jesus. The Christian church has never lacked an ample supply of theological opinions and ideas. Diversity is to be expected. But today we stand in awe of this rabbi who cared more for truth and his influence as a professional than for his own personal reputation and honor. He did not hesitate to make himself vulnerable, to go back to his Pharisee friends as a changed man, and to support an unpopular idea. More important, though, Nicodemus stopped teaching or testing his private theories on people who trusted him. Discipleship demands responsibility for its influence and spiritual stewardship. Nicodemus gave up his pet ideas in favor of truth for both his own sake and for the sake of those in his charge.

3. Lesson About the Fans

Powerful leaders and great teachers always have their followers. Such enthusiasts press around their idols, cheer and clap, collect autographs, and shower them with compliments. They want to be seen in public with the celebrities, have pictures taken shaking hands with them, and try to imitate their every move.

Jesus had His share of such admirers. What is characteristic about such people is their number and their unpredictability. They come invited by their friends, and by their sheer mass they impress onlookers and the passers-by. Imagine some of the other teachers in Jesus' time, those who could not heal or keep their audiences spellbound for hours. How would you feel in their sandals? You have three brave souls with you, and over there Jesus has a multitude. It might tempt you to quit.

Today the Master teaches us how to handle such people. "Jesus did not trust himself to them" (John 2:24). He sees them, hears their cheering, waves back to them, but that is all. If they want to follow, if they do not disturb His work, it causes no harm. But their noise, flattery, and clapping do not reach His soul. Jesus warns us to be prudent around them and not trust ourselves in their hands. Our self-confidence, our self-worth, our work must not depend on the fickleness of any fans we might have. They are easily swayed to shout "Hosanna" ("Save me" in Aramaic) one day and chant "Crucify Him!" the next.

Now, such people are more than crazy noisemakers who shout and scream for anything. They look hard for evidence of extraordinary happenings, such as healing, exorcism, or the feeding of the great multitudes. They expect you to perform, to be interesting, every single day.

That is why Jesus recommends to us individuals such as Nicodemus. In their presence He can speak and be heard or share His thoughts and be understood. His words can create new hearts and new minds. And when such encounters come to a close, He can look back and say again: "It is very good" (see Gen. 1:31).

4. LESSON ABOUT CHANGE

The first lesson facing Nicodemus takes the form of an indirect self-examination. When all the lectures are over, when a degree has been conferred, when the awards are won, the question Jesus asks is not "What do you remember?" or "What is your opinion on . . . ?" Instead, He tries to find if the knowledge of His Word produces Christlikeness, if learning about spirituality engenders a spiritual being, and if the lessons about God yield Godlikeness. With fans He chats about things, but with disciples He probes the mysteries of regeneration, the new birth.

Notice that even Nicodemus first addresses Jesus as a fan. "We know that you are a teacher come from God; for no one can do these signs that you do, unless God is with him" (John 3:2). But Jesus expects the rabbi to rise higher than just fandom. The Master is concerned about what happens inside of His disciples' minds and hearts. The Messianic work of salvation begins with hearing Him. It starts the very moment a teacher of the gospel shares the good news. The coming kingdom of God is not something that we await in some more or less distant future. It is "You must be born again." The message, and the power of the Spirit that accompanies it, has to radically change everyone, both teacher and students, *now*. The work of sanctification begins on contact with the message if the hearers and teachers yield themselves to the Spirit. Sin cannot remain comfortable and cozy for even a moment in the presence of the gospel.

5. LESSON ABOUT THE GOSPEL'S POWER

The sin problem is not just a wrinkle that we can iron out, a spot that we can clean or cover up. A human soul affected by it cannot be "repaired." I own an expensive and beautiful shirt that a friend of mine once gave to me. I always wear it to my class when I lecture on the nature of sin. At one point in my lecture I show the students the left sleeve of the shirt, on which they notice a mark. "What should I do with this spot?" I ask.

"Take it to the cleaners, Doc," comes the answer.

"No, my friend, it would not do," I reply. "You see, this is not a blemish; it is a hole burned through by a spark from my woodstove. It looks like a stain, but it is more, much more than that. To repair it I need to find a way of reconnecting the fibers of the material that the spark severed. I cannot do that. The fire destroyed them."

That's sin's effect on our inner being. It does not just stain, but destroys. Nothing short of a new creation, of regeneration, can repair Nicodemus. "You must be redone, man, re-created, not just repaired. Redone from inside out. The same Spirit that gives life can bring the 'newness of life.' It's as radical as a death and resurrection experience" (see Rom. 6:3, 4).

"Are you a teacher of Israel, and yet you do not understand this?" (John 3:10). "Do you think I would have come from God just to entertain people, to inform them of some Utopia when by-and-by My dream kingdom materializes? Do you think these signs are the focus and the goal of My ministry? Or do you think that these miracles authenticate Me as a teacher come from God? No, Nicodemus. You are the teacher of Israel. You must know that My kingdom begins now. Inside of you. You are My proof."

6. Lesson of Love From the Serpent

"And as Moses lifted up the serpent in the wilderness, so must the Son of man be lifted up, that whoever believes in him may have eternal life" (John 3:14, 15).

The hardest lesson comes at the end. Jesus is the Messiah—Nicodemus has very little doubt about that by now. What is changing in his mind, though, is his concept of the real nature of the Messiah's mission. Finally Nicodemus can see that Jesus' task is not a political, economic, or nationalistic liberation from Roman occupation. In fact, His kingdom is not of this world. He is not a universally accepted ruler yet. For a time He must be "lifted up." But that does not mean that He will be enthroned above their heads. No, at least not yet.

What Nicodemus heard troubled him greatly: Like the bronze serpent that Moses raised in the wilderness to give healing and life to those who looked up in faith, so it must be with this Master. The Pharisee had heard the serpent story from childhood. Neither he nor his teachers knew exactly what to make of it. Various theories of interpretation struggled to make sense of the event, but no one yet connected the work of the Messiah to a serpent that saves. All of this sounded utterly confusing, if not scandalous, for at least two reasons. First, if Jesus spoke Aramaic, the expression to "lift up" could also mean "to crucify." Was the Master alluding to the possibility that on the way to victory He would have to suffer crucifixion? How could He save His people if He died in such disgrace?

The second cause of perplexity was Jesus' application of the symbol of the serpent to Himself. In Hebrew and even later Christian literature the serpent stands for evil (Gen. 3:1; 13; 2 Cor. 11:3; Rev. 12:9). How could anything evil represent the Lord's Anointed? What did He have in common with the serpent?

The answer to his dilemma appears in what I think are the final words of the conversation recorded in John 3:16-21. The inauguration of the kingdom of God requires total annihilation of sin and evil. Jesus' first and foremost task is to defeat the works of the devil, and according to divine wisdom that is possible only through the sinless life and substitutionary death and resurrection of the Messiah. Nicodemus must have remembered the words of Isaiah 53 as he listened intently to Jesus. Verses 10 and 11 are especially relevant: "Yet it was the will of the Lord to bruise him; he has put him to grief; when he makes himself an offering for sin, he shall see his offspring, he shall prolong his days; the will of the Lord shall prosper in his hand; he shall see the fruit of the travail of his soul and be satisfied."

The lesson of love represented by the serpent is simply that only Jesus can open the gate of the kingdom to human beings. No human skills, disciplines, habits, or training can make us so irresistible, so good, that it assures our place in His kingdom. Nicodemus has to admit that his power and influence are useless here. He must let the Messiah become a scandal—a serpent. Jesus must become the likeness of sinful flesh, though without sin. "The evil of sin was seen in him conspicuously revealed, but conquered; not only conquered, but transformed into a remedy."* The poison of sin that would certainly kill Nicodemus and the rest of us sinners became in Jesus, the sinless One, the only antivenom available to those who believe. The sin assumed by Jesus did not conquer Him, but rather it produced in Him antibodies to itself. Nicodemus now regarded this Man as something infinitely priceless, as someone who must be protected as much as possible so His work prospers—or all of humanity is doomed.

I see Jesus and Nicodemus depart, their minds and souls united as one. "What love, what awesome love," the sleepless Nicodemus exclaims that night. Yes, we must agree, what a love!

Meaning of Discipleship

The distance Nicodemus has traveled with Jesus in such a short period of time staggers us. This chapter cannot even highlight all the lessons concealed in the night encounter; much less can we illustrate how to apply them all to our present situation. But we must mention several insights into the meaning of discipleship.

First, we find again the constant human readiness to organize God, the desire to sway Him as to His priorities. It is amazing how very few could give up their preconceived notions about Jesus, and how many missed Him completely. "It is not like God to say this . . . ," we comment today. And when the Bible touches some sensitive spot in our life, we may try to interpret the passage in a more soothing way. Yet to be a disciple of Jesus in this postmodern age means *to take God at His word and, like Nicodemus, hear Him out. Discipleship means humility so we can learn from the Master.*

Second, there exist few individuals more dangerous among us than those who are compulsory teachers. We like to tell others our version of what happened, offer our own perspective on some important issue of life. When it comes to the interpretation of some prophecy or difficult passage in Scripture, we hear dozens of opinions, and all of them claim to be final. For example, according to a friend of mine, I should not bother writing this, since the year 2000 is only a few months away and he believes that Christ will return then. Many are the teachers, and many more their followers, and ultimately countless the disillusioned people when a theory does not prove true. Experimenting on live subjects in medicine is a crime. *Discipleship today calls for an even greater sense of responsibility when we deal with human minds and lives. We need even more humility when we teach eternal truths. We should never test pet ideas on our students or fellow church members. Nicodemus teaches us to abandon them if we discover that God's Word cannot back us up completely.*

Third, it might be time to examine ourselves: Am I a fan or a disciple? Outwardly no one can see the difference, but we know what lurks inside us. Does our pastor have to be funny and interesting all the time? Is our religious life boring? Do we need to feel accepted, loved, and supported, or do we enjoy accepting, loving, and supporting others? Is my church doing for me and to me what I expect it to do, or do I serve the needs of others? If our concerns center on ourselves—our needs only—we may well be on our way to becoming fans of Jesus who admire Him as long as He is powerful and useful.

The Son of man came not to be served but to serve others, and His follower cannot do otherwise. My church should not have to organize parties, potlucks, and excursions in order to retain me. *Discipleship means readiness to give, to care, to serve Jesus when He is not popular, interesting, or famous. True discipleship begins the moment the hero worship ends.*

Fourth, nothing can replace personal *adult* relationship with Jesus. I say "adult" because many of us fear to step out of that mode of existence in which others think or decide for us. Mama cleaned and dressed my wounds, fed my tummy, washed my clothes, and kissed me all over; Papa supplied money, clothing, a bike, and unforgettable vacations, and all of that for nothing in return. They did everything just because they loved me. And now that I am outside of my parental home, I need a big heavenly Daddy who will be there when I need Him, answer when I call, overlook when I sin and hurt others, ask no questions, and neither expect nor give me responsibilities. That kind of relationship follows Judas's example, because the moment Daddy does not answer, does not perform, or will not give me the toy I crave, I too might just betray Him.

Nicodemus' example tells us that *discipleship means coming close, letting Jesus inside our comfort zone, and making sure He is comfortable enough to stay and sup with us.* The distance learning mode is not a part of the School of Jesus. One-on-one vulnerability works miracles and gives Him freedom to answer our needs as He sees fit.

———

* H. R. Reynolds, *The Gospel of St. John,* The Pulpit Commentary, ed. H.D.M. Spence and Joseph S. Exell (Grand Rapids: Eerdmans, 1950), vol. 17, p. 121.

CHAPTER 6

The Catch

FISHER OF MEN

Early in the morning four fishermen dock their two boats. A beautiful and quiet day greets their arrival. The still waters of the Sea of Galilee reflect the warm rays of the sun, while the town begins stirring after a long night.

The four men do not say anything. Their slow movements and silence betray fatigue and . . . no catch. Since they have no fish to unload, they begin to clean and mend their nets. A whole night and nothing to show for it. Nothing except some debris in their nets and some sweat. Yet, being experts at fishing, they know the lake's waters. They know when, how, and where to cast their nets. What could be the matter when time after time the men find nothing? Empty nets yield empty boats, empty pockets, empty stomachs, and empty hearts.

Ah, for some deep shade under a fig tree, and a few good hours of sleep to forget and recuperate.

Instead they hear the voices of people approaching. It must be Jesus. The four, Simon Peter, Andrew, James, and John, prefer to remain part-time students for now. They follow Jesus only occasionally. Unlike Levi, the son of Alpheus, these men need more time, and the Teacher waits for their decision.

No sooner have the crowds arrived than Jesus begins to teach. The people push and press to hear every word; to be as close as possible. And, as is often the case in a crowd, those behind do not see how far is too far to push. So Jesus finds a solution. "Getting into one of the boats, which was Simon's, he asked him to put out a little from the land. And he sat down and taught the people from the boat" (Luke 5:3). In the process Peter finds himself stuck in it with Jesus, while Andrew has to finish the task of cleaning and mending the nets.

In time the lecture ends. The next few seconds jolt Simon Peter into full wakefulness when Jesus speaks to him: " 'Put out into the deep and let down your nets for a catch.' And Simon answered, 'Master, we toiled all night and took nothing'" (verses 4, 5).

What now? Should he inform Jesus about the behavior of fish? There is no way this new fishing expedition can work. Jesus knows carpentry and most certainly is an expert in His trade. Peter, on the contrary, knows little of carpentry, but when it comes to fishing— that's another story. He is convinced that one just does not catch fish in the Sea of Galilee during broad daylight. Centuries of experience have confirmed this fact.

Besides, reputations are at stake—his own as well as those of his associates, the Zebedees. Can you imagine what people would say? If Jesus tries to cast the nets just for fun or something, the villagers and neighbors might enjoy seeing Him practice the moves. But Simon cannot afford such a thing. His instincts shout a resounding *no!*

Then another thought crosses his mind. He recalls the wedding in Cana: Jesus is not a winemaker, yet He made wine from water. And what about the demoniac in Capernaum, and his own mother-in-law (Luke 4:31-41)? Jesus heals, and carpenters do not usually compete with physicians. When Jesus speaks with such confidence and compelling authority, it is almost impossible to resist Him. He definitely is not an ordinary teacher.

So Peter decides to do what Jesus asks. After all, it is His idea. If they don't catch any fish, perhaps there might be some important lesson to learn. It's worth the risk. "At your word I will let down the nets" (Luke 5:5).

The tired, stiff muscles obey grudgingly. The boat makes a U-turn toward the open lake. Andrew, who comes along, sits quietly, eyeing both his older brother and the Master. Slowly, almost mechanically, the nets glide into the dark waters. The same routine movements as last night and many other nights for many long years.

Suddenly the two brothers look at each other in astonishment. The nets refuse to budge. The men tug harder, but no response. Only the commotion of hundreds of glistening fish fill the men with sufficient strength to hold and pull, and hold and pull. The quick reaction of James and John saves the incredible catch from spilling back into the depths.

Both vessels precariously drag the catch to the shore. The men's minds are overloaded too. It is impossible to think coherently. They are incapable of seeing the events from a long-range perspective. Short-term ideas are all they can handle. Stunned and shaky, the fishermen stumble out of the water. Jesus looks at them and smiles, but Peter is frightened. He has heard of blessings, but this is more than he can cope with. What does one do with God's exuberance? One cannot say, "Hey, take it easy, Lord." Job was exactly right when he declared, "Who will say to him, 'What doest thou?'" (Job 9:12). This very question confronts Peter head-on. "What is happening to me? What now?"

In his confusion and fear, Peter blurts, "Depart from me, for I am a sinful man, O Lord" (Luke 5:8). Such proximity to God has a way of intimidating us—of dismantling all our human masks and defenses. Standing naked before Him, we experience our thoughts and intentions, read as an open book. "How awesome is this place!" Jacob gasped (Gen. 28:17) and "Woe is me!" Isaiah exclaimed (Isa. 6:5). A deep feeling of humility floods us, because this God who controls the fish and the sea, who holds the powers of nature in obeisance, insists on staying with us. He seeks to enter our day-to-day chores and help us a little.

Jesus understands Simon, but He does not depart. Instead He calms his fear by saying, "'Do not be afraid; henceforth you will be catching men.' And when they had brought their boats to land, they left everything and followed him" (Luke 5:10, 11).

LESSONS OF DISCIPLESHIP

Right there on the seashore we could not appreciate all the rich lessons the Teacher shared with us. Impressions too vivid and emotions too deep for expression blocked our ability to think clearly and grasp fully what really happened. Only a few days later, as we replayed the events and the conversations in our minds, could we identify the valuable insights Jesus shared with us that day.

1. LESSON IN HUMAN AWARENESS

It happened just one week after my initial visit to the United States. My fiancé completed her B.A., and I witnessed my first graduation ceremony American-style. The gowns, the pageantry, the music, and the people all impressed me. I felt totally out of place. And that's when I did it: I embarrassed myself, my fiancé, my future parents-in-law, my ancestors, and my posterity. At least, that's how it felt then.

But listen. My knowledge of English and of American etiquette was little more than embryonic. As all those people, those doctors and their wives, came to shake my hand, most of them asked, "How do you do?" Their consideration touched me. Well, frankly, I felt confused, a bit tired, and extremely hot. So I told them that as best I knew how. When my fiancé explained to me in French that "How do you do?" amounts to little more than a polite "Hi," I felt crushed, betrayed, and tricked. *This must be the most uncaring expression of care there is,* I thought. *It's just a chocolate coating around a puff of hot air.*

Other languages and cultures have similar formalities. One should simply learn their meaning and adjust accordingly. More important, though, one must avoid letting formality replace genuine concern for others.

"How are you?" I said to someone a few minutes later.

"Not so good," the person replied.

"Oh, I'm so glad!"

In a hurry, without thinking, I expressed my happiness that someone felt bad, then went on my merry way like the priest hustling to Jericho.

Here along the shore of Galilee Jesus imparts the lesson of human compassion and care. The four disciples suffer from more than lack of sleep and empty net syndrome. John the Baptist, their beloved teacher, was in prison at this time. Devastated and disoriented, they question everything: the promise of the coming Messiah, their discipleship, even their belief in divine care. The beautiful thing is that Jesus knows this. At the precise moment when the vacant nets threaten to empty the disciples' lives of purpose and meaning, Jesus fills them to the brim—both the nets and their lives.

While in the wilderness we learned caution and prudence with our needs, but here at the lake we find ourselves convinced that no genuine lack, no matter how carefully concealed, will remain unanswered. Our Master will supply all of our needs (Phil. 4:19), yet with no hooks or strings attached.

2. Lesson About Growth

First Jesus asks Peter to "put out a little"—a simple and easy request and a matter of courtesy to help a friend in need. The boat becomes a lectern from which the divine teacher imparts eternal truths. However, it is not the end of the story. Before stepping onto the shore, Jesus addresses Peter again, but this time it is not a request. "Put out into the deep," He commands, and the boat becomes a stage for a miracle.

Careful and understanding with grown-up, experienced people, and gentle with small children, Jesus scrupulously measures the right dosage of involvement and challenge. "He will feed his flock like a shepherd, he will gather the lambs in his arms, he will carry them in his bosom, and gently lead those that are with young" (Isa. 40:11). All throughout the Bible God shows this same sensitivity to different stages of maturity for every individual He deals with. He did not ask Abraham to leave Ur of Chaldea while at the same time telling him that several decades later he should be ready to sacrifice his son on Mount Moriah. I wonder if Abraham would have chosen to follow God's prompting at that stage of his faith. Instead God nurtured Abraham and became his Friend. Only later, when the patriarch had grown enough, did He confront His old friend with the ultimate test of loyalty.

Today we learn not to despair over our slowness to learn and advance. Discipleship of Christ allows for growth and for learning time. It is a training experience. The character of a disciple's first steps of following cannot be the measure of his or her achievement and potential. If a college student knew everything about a subject on the first day of class, attendance at any further lectures would make no sense. No one begins with a dissertation or final exam. That fact implies that Christ's disciples are not perfect people. They are growing, learning men and women.

We are bound to make mistakes and embarrass Him. Unfortunately for Him, some lessons that we need to grasp can be acquired only at enormous cost to Him. We do not just learn *from* Him, we learn *at His expense*. He knows that, and yet He patiently spends Himself for us, just as every good teacher does, because He can see in us infinite possibilities for growth.

3. IN THE SAME BOAT WITH JESUS

As soon as Jesus steps into Peter's boat, things change. Because of His presence, the most ordinary way of casting a net, at the most unlikely time, brings results that surpass all our expectation. Human skills become exceptionally effective. What needs to be done can happen either by ordinary or extraordinary means.

Yet Peter feels puzzled. He wonders where to draw the line between faith and presumption. He is a realist, not a mystic. In the real world things are more predictable. It is true that sometimes you may spend the whole night fishing without results. But such events are normal. With Jesus in charge, the surprises are literally wonderful—or terrible—*because you have no control over them.* You cannot always say when or how He will respond to your requests. Nor can you schedule a miracle. Announcements on the radio or television that summon people to come witness God's intervention "at 6:00 p.m. tonight" have always bothered me. In reality, true miracles are amazing not only because they defy natural laws, but also because they surprise us. They pop up in the most startling places, and they do not happen where you would expect them. The conditions under which miracles take place remain a mystery to us. You can be sure only that He will help you better than anyone else at a time and in a way that He sees fit—the time and the way that is best for you. And when that is, only He knows.

So here in the boat we learn that we must reexamine our ideas of what is possible or impossible if we want Jesus to take charge of our day-to-day living. The danger we constantly face is to impose our experiences and our limits on Him. One vital lesson He wants us to learn is that His work begins where human wisdom and know-how capitulate, and from a human perspective, this may involve fishing at midday and looking foolish until the catch is in. In the case of Peter's fishing, the results came rapidly. The boats pulled to shore, loaded to overflowing, and the catch was clearly visible to those who lingered on the shore. But it may not always be so.

4. FISHER OF MEN

While the disciples hesitated to spread their nets, while they worked laboriously, while the nets refused to budge and the boats threatened to sink from the weight of fish in them, another more important fishing event also took place. Jesus tried to reach His disciples' hearts. He wished that they could trust Him more completely—more than their nets and their profession. Jesus sought to win them away from their reliance on commercial and material fortunes. To accomplish this, He became involved in their lives in a more tangible way.

With Jesus in the boat, the extraordinary invaded the intimacy of personal existence. Peter had heard of Moriah, the Red Sea, the manna, the walls of Jericho, Mount Carmel, and the lions' den. The heroic history of his people pulsated in his veins and gave him a strong sense of identity. But the miracle here is something else. Look at this catch. All the fish! All the capital! This is Peter's boat. He knows every board in it. It is his everyday workplace, as comfortable as an old shoe. But he is dazed, unable to deny the miracle. What has happened to him is not just another fish story, nor is it almost legendary like Jericho or Mount Carmel. The event has touched him directly and intimately. Peter gives in and gives himself up. He is caught. God has him firmly in His hands. What a secure place to be!

5. LESSON IN STEADFASTNESS

Such personal experiences with God have their price. Moments before Jesus steps inside his boat, Peter is tempted to shelter his life within the confines of a low-risk existence. He begins to see himself as an average guy, earning his living and managing his family as best he can, and like many others, waiting passively for the coming Messiah. He must make himself comfortable with such a life—especially now, with John the Baptist imprisoned.

In his younger years Peter had ambitions. He had felt sure there was a better way to avoid mistakes and maximize profit. If only he could have a chance at it. Then his time came. Not satisfied with little things done in the same old way, he contracted to supply fish for some wealthy individual who owned fishing rights. Later, hearing of John the Baptist, Peter went to hear him. Convinced of the genuineness and relevance of John's message, Peter became one of his disciples, constantly learning and always seeking to understand God's unsearchable wisdom.

But now, in his mature years, Peter had tasted disappointment and failure. The fishing disaster last night just revived in him the ever-present fear of total collapse so familiar in the life of a contract fishing business. In addition, God's silence when his teacher, John the Baptist, needed protection now threatened to engulf his desire for a more meaningful relationship with this God.

And then the miracle came. It left Peter confused for a while. Matthew and Mark show Jesus walking by the sea, probably later that day. Seeing the men with their nets, He tells them, "Follow me" (Matt. 4:18-22; Mark 1:16-20).

Peter cannot resist anymore. Experiencing Jesus' invitation as a call of destiny, he hears the new Teacher saying to him, "Come, Peter. Come out again. Only this time, leave the comfort zone of an average existence and risk your life with Me. See for yourself that only the ultimate sacrifice for Me can bring ultimate meaning to your life. Only this kind of steadfast commitment to follow Me can overcome your primeval fear of failure and death." And Peter follows.

MEANING OF DISCIPLESHIP

Centuries have passed, but the story of the miraculous fishing still speaks meaningfully to the contemporary scene.

First, to follow Jesus means to admit Him inside our boat—our daily struggles, boredom, fears, and joys. Impersonal, distant discipleship is a contradiction in terms. Theoretical and formal profession of faith stands miles apart from Him. Discipleship is not a heritage handed down from parents to children or from a culture to its posterity. Christian homes and Christian churches have a unique function in transmitting the Christlike worldview and Christian lifestyle. But no amount of persuasion, investment of time and energy, modeling, prayer, and even love can guarantee our son's or daughter's commitment to Him. Our covenant is ours alone.

One day Jesus will most certainly come to my and your "boat," and to the "boat" of my son and your daughter, searching for a place to sit down and teach. Such events are not social in nature. Private and personal, they do not demand public witness or approval. Your and my autonomous will has the sovereign power over the decision to let Him in. We do not know how many opportunities we will have—only that He chooses people every day. That "if any one hears my voice and opens the door, I will come in to him, and eat with him and he with me" (Rev. 3:20). *Discipleship means a one-on-one interface with Jesus.*

Second, we would do well to realize that as Teacher, Jesus is our leader. During the first months of my work in North America I made an appointment to see the president of my employing conference. After some informal chatting, I decided to focus on the main subject of my visit. Feeling comfortable with the situation, I said something like this: "Sir, I wish to demand permission to study for my doctorate in ethics at McGill University here in town." To my surprise, both the president and secretary-treasurer looked uncomfortable. *What kind of rudeness is this?* they must have thought. Then, regaining his composure, the president said, "Miroslav, luckily for you I know French. The word *demander* in French means 'to request.' In English, my dear friend, it is emphatic. Very emphatic. Too emphatic for you to get anywhere when you 'demand.' I understand your intentions, though. Let's explore the possibilities."

Once Jesus enters our private life, He offers us His insight and help. As Teacher, He is not the one who receives instruction and orders such as "Jesus, take care of my kids, help me with exams, protect my husband on the road, give me health." We can express such things in a mode of supplication, but they can easily become demands if not even commands—all listed in order of our preference. Instead, Jesus takes charge, not because by nature He is bossy, but because our position on the map of life is far too distant from home and we have no time to waste. *Discipleship means readiness to obey.*

Third, every day with Jesus carries the possibility of challenges to our comfort zone. Each time a thesis defense comes around, I have a frightened candidate on my hands. As mentor, I have watched my student's progress and maturation. "Do you think I can do this?" they ask. The student is never sure. They always have an acute awareness that only God in heaven knows everything. With my assurances and coaching, though, they take on the questions and succeed.

Jesus gives us time, space, and room to grow. Only He can realistically judge our readiness for diverse challenges. From the proximity of a close friendship with us He may ask us to climb Moriah or Horeb or Zion. One thing is sure: He will not ask us to mount the hill of Calvary. He passed that exam for us and transferred His credits to our transcript. With the assurance that He can measure our readiness and that Calvary is out of the question, *discipleship means trusting in His wisdom.*

Fourth, Simon has learned to act his obedience. How many times have we missed important opportunities because of our inaction on issues that matter. Sloth, along with pride, lies at the foundation of all sin. G. A. Chadwick observes that "how many are the invertebrate souls, lacking in will and void of purpose, who, instead of piercing waves and conquering the flow of adverse tides, like mendusae, can only drift, all limp and languid, in the current of circumstance! Such men do not make apostles; they are but ciphers of flesh and blood, of no value by themselves, and only of any worth as they are attached to the unit of some stronger will. A poor broken thing is a life spent in the subjunctive mood, among the 'mights' and 'shoulds,' where the 'I will' waits upon 'I would.'"[*]

Fifth, as the training of the will advances, a disciple becomes stronger and more prepared to reflect the Master's will, just as the actions of a well-prepared soldier reflect the will of the officer.

The captain of our platoon enjoyed the respect of the entire battalion. If the colonel wanted song, march, parade, or some other performance, he needed only to put Captain Knezevic in charge. The officer respected every soldier, cared for and defended their basic needs—but then he expected willing cooperation. Rare were those who would not become deaf to everything else, even the voice of danger and death, if Captain Knezevic issued an order.

"Do whatever he tells you," Mary advised the servants at Cana in Galiliee (John 2:5). "Do whatever." Give Him carte blanche. "At your word," Peter concedes, and a miracle happens.

He who decides to give priority to the will of the Master will taste wine where others drink water, and find fish where most discover seaweed. *Discipleship means readiness to act at His word.*

Sixth, discipleship contradicts our quick-fix, fast-food mentality. It means growth. No amount of pushing or pulling can mature either carrots *or* characters. Unlike the social and political revolutions in our history, the forces of heaven move softly and slowly, lighting up our horizon gradually, lest a sudden revelation should dazzle and blind us or the whole weight of duty fall at once on our shoulders and drive us to despair.

At times we have much less patience with ourselves, our spouses, our kids, our fellow church members, our pastors, our conference presidents, than Jesus does. The growth in grace seems so slow! One experience, one failure, one sermon delivered loudly and cogently with biblical support, does not seem to teach the lesson, and we become discouraged. But the Master has no use for force or intimidation. "Let it alone, sir, this year also," He pleads with undauntable tenacity (Luke 13:8). *Discipleship means letting Jesus take all the time He needs to nurture us to maturity.*

Finally, the life of discipleship is not an end in itself. Jesus tried to win the hearts of these fishermen not simply because His job and reputation required Him to enlist a respectable number of students. Nor do disciples follow Him simply because they are lost and He knows the way better than anyone else. Jesus enters your boat and mine, He manifests His presence, He intervenes on our behalf when no one else could help, because of the family, relatives, neighbors, and strangers on our life's path. To those who inquire, "Sir, we wish to see

Jesus" (John 12:21), He needs us to say what Andrew told Peter: "We have found the Messiah" (John 1:41). This is it, everybody! Search no more. He is *it!*

To the people around us, Jesus is invisible, but we see Him by faith. Most of our contemporaries think He is an absent Lord, if He is Lord at all. But we have deep personal experience of His presence. Many people wonder and search, listening to the gurus of the day, but we have found the Master. And because they cannot see Him, Jesus needs us, His visible, audible, touchable extensions of Himself. We are the proof of His existence and trustworthiness. If we must "fish" for a living, we must also be "fishers of men." *Discipleship means leading others to find the Way.*

---

* Henry Burton, *The Gospel According to St. Luke, The Expositor's Bible,* ed. W. Robertson Nicoll (New York: A. C. Armstrong and Son, 1908), vol. 16, pp. 167, 168.

CHAPTER 7

LEFT IN THE LURCH

Wait, wait, you herd of peasants! All of you will get your ration."

Wait we did. Since early that morning my mom and I had stood in the line, expecting our portion of flour and powdered eggs provided by the U.S.A.

Peasants we were, too—cold, starving, ill-clad farmers. I watched the others as I waited, my toes freezing. Faint puffs of breath escaped from each mouth. On the tip of every nose hung a drop of rain, and no one bothered about it. We didn't have handkerchiefs, and our soaking sleeves were of no use in wiping our faces.

Umbrellas? Only the comerad had one. You see, although born and raised in the same village, only three months ago he had managed to join the higher "caste." Because of the red star on his fur hat he did not have to wear wooden or peasant shoes. He boasted real leather boots. Even the buttons on his imposing trench coat displayed a red star. At times I caught myself staring at him in a mixture of admiration and fear.

"You all will get your allowance, and that's a guarantee," he would repeat with the self-assurance of a wet-behind-the-ears zealot. But no one believed him. Especially not when around 8:00 that morning a tractor with an empty trailer entered the gate and a few minutes later, in plain sight, departed with a load. We all knew where most of the United Nations relief shipment went. Tomorrow those who had some money could buy it on the black market.

As for us, we all got less than half of the promised supplies.

"What happened to the rest?" the "peasants" demanded.

"That's all we have for now. Here, come and see for yourselves," the official answered.

My experience from my childhood years, one of myriads like it, depicts the life of the poor, the marginalized masses of the world. The life of those punished for their honesty by the corrupt; the misery of those exploited for their hard work by the "liberators." Worst of all, it is an existence with no hope for the future, an injustice without appeal.

But wait. Come with me to meet Jairus. See what will happen to him today. We read in Luke 8:40-42, 49 that a "ruler of the synagogue" comes to your and my Master and falls at His feet, beseeching Him to hasten to his house, "for he had an only daughter, about twelve years of age, and she was dying." It was an urgent request. You imagine the Master jumping on the fastest donkey available, with Jairus running ahead screaming and shoving the milling crowds out of the way. As you see the people watching with awe the Master's eagerness to help this good, respectable man, you sense their feeling of security as they become aware of this extraordinary medical service at their disposal. Would you delay such an errand? Would you slowly tie your shoelaces or comb your hair first before responding? Of course not!

Well, Jesus does start out with Jairus, but the curious crowd slows the dash to a crawl until Jesus suddenly stops. The father, whose expression alternates between fear and peace, worry and hope, frown and smile—whose feet, elbows, and shoulders eagerly plow ahead—suddenly finds himself abandoned.

What's happened now? he must have thought. *What could possibly be more important, more urgent? If He only knew my daughter's true condition: her face emaciated, her eyes sunken, her pleading voice and heavy breath. What is it that stopped Him? Did I not make my plea urgent enough? Maybe I am not worthy of His help.*

Then he learns that a woman suffering from a chronic hemorrhage has touched Jesus. So He stops. She has rendered Him ceremonially unclean (Lev. 15:25-27). Can He not take care of this later—after He first heals the dying daughter? Who would give priority to a chronic rather than an acute case? Should He really bother with the cultic regulations of cleanliness now, at just this moment? After all, Jesus does not hesitate to touch the lepers! Besides, He knows that the sons of Zebedee, John and James, together with the crowd, can take care of the woman.

Then the final blow hits without mercy. "Your daughter is dead," a servant notifies him.

Jairus stares at the man as though in a daze. His soul is numb. "Do not trouble the Teacher any more," concludes the messenger sadly (Luke 8:49).

He is right! Absolutely right. Why trouble Him now? I should have remained at the bedside, holding my daughter's hand. Tears flow freely. Who cares what others would say? "May as well go now. My wife—her grief. I must tell her why we did not come sooner. I did run—as fast as I could. I did my honest best. I guess I just do not get it, Master!"

But Jesus catches the words, though spoken softly.[*] He too senses the heaviness, the darkness, the hopelessness. He spots the flickering flame of the fainting father's faith: "Do not fear; only believe, and she will be well," He tells the man (verse 50).

"Believe, and she shall be well." The two—faith and healing—side by side? My faith and her health in a cause-and-effect relationship? I thought that if I prayed He would tackle the case alone and that I had better get out of the way.

Believe—well, that's easy to say. Before she died, His healing power—the same that made this bleeding woman well—could have saved her. But now that is not enough. How can she be well and dead at the same time?

Now Jesus hurries. The cries and wailing lead him to Jairus's house. As He reaches it He calls Peter, James, and John to accompany Him, and interrupts the wailing with the words "Do not weep; for she is not dead but sleeping" (verse 52). But they do not impress family, friends, and neighbors. They have seen the girl's condition and He has not. What kind of physician does He think He is? Diagnosis without examination? Instead the noise becomes even more irritating. "They laughed at him, knowing that she was dead" (verse 53).

With the power and dignity of a Master "he put them all outside, and took the child's father and mother and those who were with him, and went in where the child was" (Mark 5:40). At this point all the tumult ceases. The wailers, the flute players, the mourners all hush. They all strain to see or hear what is going on inside the room.

Mark informs us that Jesus simply took the lifeless hand of the deceased and called to her gently. The Word spoke the words that dead ears could do no else but hear. " 'Talitha cumi'; which means, 'Little girl, I say to you, arise.' And immediately the girl got up and walked (she was twelve years of age), and they were immediately overcome with amazement. And he strictly charged them that no one should know this, and told them to give her something to eat" (verses 41-43).

LESSONS OF DISCIPLESHIP

To live the event as it unfolds, without an awareness of its final outcome, as in the case of Jairus, creates a series of serious questions. Why did Jesus let anything delay Him? What determines His priorities? What makes God's timing in responding to our needs different from ours? Such questions were real to Jairus just as they are to us. As we learn the following lessons several answers emerge.

1. LESSONS OF FAITH

It appears, at closer scrutiny, that neither Jairus, his daughter, nor the woman with the hemorrhage occupies center stage of this story. Jesus' attention is on faith. "Only believe," He urges the father.

Believe what? Believe that Jesus can heal? Jairus expressed his faith in healing by seeking Jesus' help. Besides, healing cannot be the issue in question now, since Jesus addresses His encouraging words after the child has already died. More important, though, a faith that counts only on what Jesus can do for us runs the risk of self-defeat. The omnipotent God *can* do much more that He *will* actually do. It means that it is not my faith in His ability to answer my petition that *moves Him to action*. Rather, it is my faith in who He is that makes the difference. To center my trust in God's capacity to help could possibly hurt my faith if He chooses, in His infinite wisdom, not to intervene.

The father now faces death, not sickness, and to Jairus death is an end to all possible action. That is why Jesus expects from Jairus a new and different kind of faith—faith in the *Person,* not merely in His *actions.* There is nothing more to do now—there is only a Person. Jairus can lean only on Jesus and not on His reputation as a healer. He must make a gigantic jump from *believing in Jesus' power* to *believing Jesus* in the use of that power. He must believe Him even to the point of death—death not his own but something worse yet: the death of his child. Faith that does not depend on divine performance says, "Though he slay me, yet will I trust in him" (Job 13:15, KJV). It trusts not because of, but rather in spite of, evidence. It bases its faith not on the evidence, but rather on the Person.

2. Lesson of Time and the Ultimate

If only we could enter Jairus's mind earlier as he waited for the Master to come by, as he counted the long seconds. Of course, he has no right, no contract, with Jesus to lay claim on His services. He stands stretched between the urgency of a real need and the presence of this inscrutable, awesome, equally real Man. Jairus could explain, even complain to Jesus about his plight, but Jesus' eyes and His face communicate understanding and compassion so clearly and so completely that the official finds himself at a loss for words. A common sense, a common humanity, a common plight, and a common mortality with Jesus encourages him that no tragic delay will occur. Now that he has found Him and told Him his need, the child must be safe.

Yet time for Jairus flies at a faster pace than ever. With consternation he realizes that even the Master cannot keep up with him as he shoves his way through the crowded streets. And when he hears the news of his daughter's death, in that instant time stops. The events, the sense of urgency—all instantly lose any meaning. It is as if Jesus' clock no longer follows the movement of the sun He created. Or as if the human fear of death cannot reach Him, and consequently no real urgency exists for Him. A life that truly overcomes the fear of death has no deadlines.

Jairus seems to understand all of this in some hazy, inarticulate, disoriented way. If only he could share it with his wife, but he has no words to express it. Like Abraham facing the outrageous command to slay his son, Jairus must remain alone with his secret thoughts.

His experience teaches us this strange way of looking at the tragedies in our lives. While he cannot fully understand it, a calm confidence surrounds him in Jesus' presence. His experience teaches us that we must place ultimate tragedy into the hands of the ultimate Helper, to whom time means nothing.

3. LESSONS OF THE PRESENT

Looking at the crowd and hearing their cries (that probably intensify at Jairus's approach), Jesus makes two surprising remarks: "Why do you make a tumult and weep? The child is not dead but sleeping" (Mark 5:39).

First, such a question seems strangely out of place. It perplexes if not embarrasses us. Normal people cry when someone dies, and some parts of the world express grief with noise. It was not the first time that Jesus had seen and heard such scenes. They cry because the little girl is dead and is gone from their embrace, their lives, and their love. That hurts. And we humans cry when something hurts us.

And then, as if to confuse the people even more, Jesus claims that the girl is not dead. We can understand why the mourners begin to mock Him. His statement seems in such bad taste, such a clumsy way of handling an already tragic situation.

As for Jesus, He goes about His duties with confidence and purpose, making no apologies. The future—not history—determines His behavior. He acts as if the child is not really dead but just taking a snooze. Jesus has directed His remark toward the future, not the past. It is prognosis, not diagnosis. Her state is sleep and not death because of what Jesus intends to do for her. In amazement we learn with Jairus that the advent of Jesus has broken the ultimacy of death. The future is now, and happiest are those who live by that future.

4. LESSONS OF WHOLENESS

Try to picture Jesus holding the pale hand of your own daughter, ordering her to rise. Notice the color returning to her skin, her eyes opening. Sitting up, she looks around and wonders at all the people crowding the room, all but one with amazement in their expressions. Cautiously she stands up and makes a few steps toward you. What would you do? I cannot imagine you, her parents, jumping and screaming and praising God. No, not yet. The whole experience is too incredible, too extraordinary, to grasp its meaning so quickly.

But Jesus wakes the parents up from their amazement when He casually orders them to feed her. She is alive, and she needs food!

Yet to us this awesome miracle, the privilege to witness His power, is a sacred moment. These are spiritual experiences! Food? Eating? That's ordinary, physical—insignificant. Resurrection is supernatural, and hunger is only natural. Who cares for the requirements of a mortal body when God is meeting the needs of our soul? Jesus does. To Him all the body's genuine needs are important. There is no virtue in neglecting the physical being in favor of the soul, because no soul exists outside of the body. And neglecting one will most certainly affect the other.

So now the crowd sees the mother emerging from the room and heading toward the kitchen area, hastily preparing her daughter's favorite dish. What an anticlimax! The kitchen—not the synagogue? Where are the chants, the "glory hallelujahs," the lighting of a candle and praying to the Master, the sprinkling of the holy water on the kneeling worshipers? No, Jesus comes out and greets Jairus, and His disciples, tight-lipped, follow Him on their way. This is our Master—the God of everyday life, the Lord and Caretaker of nature and beyond.

5. LESSONS IN DIVINE OBJECTIVITY

Finally, Jairus's experience teaches us that we are not necessarily the most important people to God, that our case may not be the most urgent, that our suffering may not be the worst possible tragedy for us, and that our God of heaven is not our private valet.

That indeed is a most difficult lesson to learn.

If we could own God as a master owns a slave, we would arrange things in a much different way. Would you not expect God to protect your father from death if you had His services? Let me take you to May 1945, just a few weeks before the end of World War II. My parents had 11 children, eight of them living and one on the way. Father had been head elder of our local congregation for 17 years and was leader of an 80-member church, the fruit of his and my mother's sacrificial witnessing efforts. Why in the name of fairness, and for the sake of his church, did he have to die when hundreds of other men—criminals and . . . Why did he have to perish?

Jairus learned that his priorities were only a part of the larger equation. Jesus is God of all. He can see clearly the lives and destinies of everyone with whom the little girl is, and will be, in contact. The Master can foresee the uses and abuses of freedom as well as the consequences of those choices. And then, placing eternity's well-being as the highest priority, He makes the hard and painful decisions—decisions that Jairus would also make if he could share His knowledge, His goodness, His courage, and His love.

The outcomes of such decisions may not always be ideal, because God does not always have our full and constant cooperation. But Jairus's example illustrates that they are the best possible strategy in the midst of the raging great controversy.

MEANING OF DISCIPLESHIP

No set of lessons could be more directly relevant today than the ones we have learned with Jairus. It bothers us that paramedics and firefighters seem to respond more quickly to the emergencies of strangers than God seems to react to the needs of His children. The fact that He is so unpredictable makes bad PR for Him, His church, and His followers. We cannot see Him now, or explain some of His present actions or inactions, and yet we must trust Him enough to follow Him. Jairus clings to Jesus. As for us, we wonder how we can remain His disciples and at the same time retain respectability today.

First, we must recognize our limited and one-sided frame of mind. We civilized people of the twenty-first century value and trust the scientific, the rational, and the left-brain mode of thinking. No matter if it is mathematics or maternity, emission control or emotion control, fact or faith, we turn to science and its child, technology, to cure our ills. Truth must make sense. Since miracles do not make sense, they belong to the realm of the paranormal. Abraham belongs in jail for child abuse and attempted murder, and Jesus should have His medical license revoked for attending to a chronic patient while letting a little girl die. Besides, we cannot analyze Jesus' methods in the scientific laboratory or replicate them at will. Most important, though, if He has the power to resurrect the dead, He is guilty of allowing fatalities when He does not immediately intervene. Physicians must do their best. Why did He resurrect Lazarus, this little girl, and the son of the widow, but not others? Why didn't He resurrect all He could possibly reach, and have put the undertakers out of business for at least the three and one-half years of His life on earth? Why does He raise only some, and on what basis?

When we deal with Jesus as teacher, as healer, and as friend, we must first guard against applying the same criteria that we would use to judge His human counterparts. We must be ready for the irrational, the mystical—yes, even what the present age regards as the paranormal. Each of us must give Him room to be God in our lives on His terms. The rational and the scientific approach restrict us to the physical and the presently observable and tend to eliminate the spiritual and divine factors that also belong to us by nature. In other words, *discipleship means regaining the full measure of the image of God in us, so as to discern aright the actions of our divine Master and enable us to follow Him.*

Second, we must ever be mindful of both our limited perspective and our bias. This results not only from our creaturely limitations, but also because of the way we know things. We learn and form our views partly from memory and experience, but mainly through information that must come from outside us. It must be fed to us by others who have their own point of view and agenda. I remember listening to BBC and Radio Moscow reports on the same event in Srebrenica, Bosnia, during the recent war there. The BBC announced the *fall* of Srebrenica. The Serbs took Muslim men by the thousands (mass graves told later of their destination and destiny), and women and children remained behind, defenseless and vulnerable to abuse and violence. One hour later Radio Moscow reported the *liberation* of Srebrenica. "The international monitors had to give in when facing the heroic liberators. The jubilant population can at last live in peace," the announcer said.

The two sources presented the same event, but gave diametrically different pictures. Because I was not there myself and seeing it all, I could not take either report at face value. I was helpless and confused about the facts of even a recent event. How much more inadequate my knowledge is of the future, the viewpoint from which Jesus acts today. And how much more accurate is the judgment of the One who knows not only what the Hitlers or Stalins of all centuries do in secret, but is also the One who reads the intentions of every heart. David expresses so eloquently God's overwhelming knowledge in Psalm 139. In verse 6 he exclaims: "Such knowledge is too wonderful for me; it is high, I cannot attain it."

Remember, much of our panic and despair comes from our not knowing the outcome as we endure trials. *Discipleship means trusting the Master, because He acts today from the perspective of our happiness and approval at the end of the road.* It must be hard to be Jesus, the Master, leading such a bunch of restless people and trying to teach us when we think we already know it all!

Third, in our Western culture, performance is the key. We choose the dishwasher, car, house, profession, and even religion that delivers the goods expected. Even a physician who holds an outstanding degree from the most reputable school fades quickly into the shadows behind the one who makes us feel well immediately. Our degree of trust corresponds directly with the degree of success.

There is nothing wrong with such reasoning unless we carry it into our relationships with our fellow humans or with the Master. What if a spouse does not match exactly our expectations? What if a son's or daughter's conduct, reputation, and lifestyle bring shame or bankruptcy? What of a child with a disability or some chronic condition? What of a Master who consistently chooses for us long-range benefits instead of immediate ones (Matt. 6:19-33), eternal results over temporal (Luke 12:13-21), or spiritual at some expense to the physical (cf. 2 Cor. 12:7-9). He will not keep justifying Himself for the immediate results, for His speed, or for His choices.

As with Jairus, we need to press closer to Him as the tragedy grows more desperate. We will trust Him, because *discipleship means staying by Him at all costs.*

Fifth, we need to discover today that Jesus treats us individually according to our unique needs. He discriminates not on the basis of color, race, or gender, but on the basis of our personal situation. When we grasp this truth, we will realize how foolish it is to compare how He treats us with His handling of others. Asaph, the other great psalmist, almost stumbled when he compared his blessings with the apparent abundance and prosperity of the ungodly (Ps. 73). Disciples before us have lived a tortuous existence, constantly trying to weigh how much attention each received and consequently, who among them was the greatest (Mark 9:33-37). Thus *discipleship means learning to genuinely rejoice in the prosperity and advancement of others, knowing that the Master will treat us right.*

---

[*] *The Seventh-day Adventist Bible Commentary* (Washington, D.C.: Review and Herald Pub. Assn., 1980), vol. 5, p. 608.

CHAPTER 8

The Outcast

TOUCHED BY A TOUCH

O ne morning a voice drifts down from a rooftop room to the people in the street below. Despite the shouts of the merchants and the brays and barks of animals, they hear a woman sobbing. Then she begins to speak to herself. They have heard it before. "Why can't I just accept God's will for me?" she demands of herself. "Why do I spend so much money and time on a fruitless search for healing? Lord, forgive me if I am arrogant, rebellious, or insubordinate, but please, give me peace. I do not know why I have been punished like this. Help me to find out how I have sinned against You."

Her name we do not know, but she must have been in her late 20s. She had been hemorrhaging for 12 years and "could not be healed by any one" (Luke 8:43). Perhaps Dr. Luke speaks too cautiously here as a physician, and we must let evangelist Mark supply us with more details: "And there was a woman who had had a flow of blood for twelve years, and who had suffered much under many physicians, and had spent all that she had, and was no better but rather grew worse" (Mark 5:25, 26).

Now, imagine her situation just for a moment.

● Constant hemorrhage without present-day disposable, hygienic supplies.

● Stifling heat, dust, flies, and scarcity of water. Not once could she afford an empty clothesline, nor could she count on a regular daily bath.

- No useful wage-earning jobs and no medical insurance.
- Perpetual pain and irritability, accompanied by anemia and fatigue.
- The whole town knew her secret, but no one ventured to speak about it, so odious was her case.
- The most difficult of all her burdens had to be her perpetual cultic uncleanliness. Moses, in his God-given wisdom, identified such people as untouchable. The ordinance was not only still valid; her religion also rigorously applied it. "If a woman has a discharge of blood for many days, not at the time of her impurity, or if she has a discharge beyond the time of her impurity, all the days of her discharge she shall continue in uncleanliness; as in the days of her impurity, she shall be unclean. Every bed on which she lies, all the days of her discharge, shall be to her as the bed of her impurity; and everything on which she sits shall be unclean, as in the uncleanliness of her impurity. And whoever touches these things shall be unclean, and shall wash his clothes, and bathe himself in water, and be unclean until the evening" (Lev. 15:25-27).

The woman knew by heart what the law said, and she accepted it. She did not try to change the church manual to fit her needs. On the streets people avoided her contact, and in the marketplace she had to stay on the margins with other outcasts. Sabbath, when she heard the prayers and chanting only from a "safe" distance, it reminded her ever anew of her lot, and her desire for healing grew stronger with every failure.

Today, as she awoke, she remembered Jesus. When she had heard about Him recently her faith had once more burst into flames underneath the ashes of her previous disappointments. Although she tried to remain cautious, she knew that she could not rest until this new healer turned His powers on her ailment. She would make another attempt. But what if . . . ?

Jesus is at the seashore teaching. During the morning hours, in the coolness of the air, He teaches—and touches and heals. Will He touch and heal her? Quickly she cleans herself more carefully than usual, because, what if . . . ? Shivers pass down her spine just at the thought of being normal. To go down the street and greet people and touch—and be touched—without any stigma of disgrace. To rejoin her rightful place in society among the women at the market, the well—the synagogue.

Heading toward the shore, her head down, she hears the rumble of the crowd. Looking up, she spots Him and stops. He is not more than a few dozen feet away from her. I cannot even imagine how I would feel! But in her case, her special case—it's so difficult always to be a special case! In her unique situation, Jesus, though close, is unreachable. *Her hope, her Healer, her new life of freedom from uncleanliness, walks surrounded by clean people!* How in the world can she get close enough to Him to be heard? She has no right to plunge into the crowd and render many of them unclean. They are her neighbors and friends who have pitied her and tolerated her presence for so long.

So she hesitates. What seems like an eternity passes. Then, just as her faith begins to faint, the incredible happens. "Christ knew every thought of her mind, and He was making His way to where she stood. He realized her great need, and He was helping her to exercise faith" *(The Ministry of Healing,* p. 60).

Can you see Jesus and the crowd veer from their course toward Jairus's house and head toward her? All of them—Jairus included! Now she has no need to push her way toward Jesus. He approaches within reach, and instinctively she touches His garment. And instantly she feels no pain, weakness, or cramps. Nothing! How wonderful it is to feel nothing; no headache, no toothache, no joints aching—nothing.

A new secret fills her heart, one that everybody will soon know and broadcast everywhere. But for now, she had better leave—and fast—and keep quiet. It's like a beautiful dream we do not want to see vanish into reality, and she feverishly, desperately, tries to preserve her newfound sense of wholeness at all cost.

But not for long. "Who was it that touched me?" she hears Him speak. Oh no! Will He discover her? All around her everyone denies it. Should she reveal what she has done? Then Peter unwittingly comes to the rescue. "Master," he says matter-of-factly, "the multitudes surround you and press upon you!" (Luke 8:45). Jesus' disciples add, "You see the crowd pressing around you, and yet you say, 'Who touched me?'" (Mark 5:31). But Jesus persists: "Some one touched me; for I perceive the power has gone forth from me" (Luke 8:46). "And he looked around to see who had done it. But the woman, knowing what had been done to her, came in fear and trembling and fell down before him, and told him the whole truth. And he said to her, 'Daughter, your faith has made you well; go in peace, and be healed of your disease'" (Mark 5:32-34).

LESSONS OF DISCIPLESHIP

With the crowd now gone we linger a while to grasp all the incident's lessons and their significance. The story appeals to all of us, because it touches the very real human problem of random suffering. A chronically ill patient spends all her money, tries all the remedies, trusts all her physicians, and finds no solution—until she touches Jesus and receives a complete restoration of health. How wonderful to witness an event with such a happy ending. But what if those of us who read the account also suffer from a debilitating condition? We too try, and we also believe, and we also wait—except that Jesus is gone, and it seems He does not hear us. What lessons of discipleship can we learn today?

1. LESSON FROM THE MARGINS

Twelve years is a long time, enough to pass through all the stages of grief until we perhaps give in and give up. Constant emotional stress leaves its toll. We can either surrender to total despair or entrust our destiny into God's hands. As we watch the woman, we learn the wisdom of making the second choice.

Her suffering and constant isolation teach her to keep her physical and social disability strictly separate from her sense of identity. She understands her limitations, and instead of begging for attention, demanding help, or imposing herself on the pity of others, she retains her dignity and respect. Her condition—not herself as a person— precludes her from a full participation in life.

At the same time she could see how Jairus approached the

Master. She knew that as he neared Jesus people probably parted and hushed, so he could have Jesus' full attention. It may not be fair, but she perceived the need for a different strategy. With all the "clean" people around Jesus noisily demanding His attention, she said to herself, "If I only touch his garment, I shall be made well" (Matt. 9:21). The woman would not force herself on Him. Nobody would need to feel that she was a burden. Not for a second would she slow Him down and endanger the life of Jairus's daughter. Also notice that at no point did she exhibit an inferiority complex or attack the taboos of her culture.

The first lesson we receive from her is that not all the rejects, the ostracized, the homeless, are hopeless in the company of this Master, nor is every silence and show of meekness a sign of weakness. Disciples are people—women or men—who like their Master willingly carry their own crosses. Not every question has to be answered, not every wrong righted, not every crime punished, and not every death avenged before they can enjoy peace in the midst of storm.

2. LESSON OF COURAGE

The woman also reveals the courage of true discipleship—the courage to stand alone. To a bystander her life might appear extremely lonely, and no doubt she really did have to face a great deal of loneliness. But with God's help she somehow learned the art of controlling and determining her own moods instead of just reacting to life's unfairness. People often mistake independence and reliance on God for loneliness. But no one can make us afraid unless we first allow them to scare us. It is our choice whether we let others offend and shame us or convince us that we really are abandoned and rejected. Unfortunately, some people have a need to hurt others and cannot feel good without using weaker and more vulnerable individuals as stepping-stones in their journey through life. But if we face such people with an independence born of God-inspired courage, instead of being destroyed by them, we might be able to minister to them.

Although accepting her lot and learning to manage her condition, the hemorrhaging woman did not passively submit to the status quo. She courageously sought healing without giving in to intimidation or retaliation. Instead, she makes a wonderfully brave move toward Jesus, and He then takes the remaining steps needed to complete her journey to a brand-new life beyond her wildest dreams.

3. POWER OF A SECRET CONNECTION

Peter and the other "clean" people are oblivious to the woman. Although they keep a good watch on everything around Jesus, Jairus and his need completely absorb their attention. Convinced that their Master can heal Jairus's daughter, the only question that lingers in their mind might be what its full effect will be on His ministry—and on themselves. He cannot miss such a good opportunity, if only for PR purposes.

This public ministry is not such a bad idea, they might have thought, *in spite of the obvious dangers caused by the jealousy of the official leadership. People can see for themselves what Jesus is all about, and no one can accuse the Master of some covert conspiracy.* Jesus will use this argument during His defense before the high priest: "I have spoken openly to the world; I have always taught in synagogues and in the temple, where all Jews come together; I have said nothing secretly" (John 18:20). Besides, I wonder how Judas and even Peter felt when the prestigious leader fell down at their Master's feet, beseeching His help.

Preoccupied with such thoughts, they did not understand why Jesus would detour on His way to Jairus's home. What had distracted Him, and where was He going?

Only Jesus and the woman knew the answer. The episode with the woman teaches us that discipleship is a public lifestyle, but that its life-changing power depends exclusively upon a personal and private connection with the Master. The woman's thoughts, her dilemma, her desperate need for His divine intervention, the phenomenal concentration of all her hopes, faith, and dreams in the secret touch of Christ's garment—none of this entered the disciples' minds. Yet according to Jesus, the only public act the woman performed—the touch itself—had no power to heal her. The disciples offered freely their testimony to that effect. Instead, Jesus says, "Your faith has made you well" (Luke 8:48). Only faith that reaches out is ever effective. Without this connection with Jesus, discipleship turns into just profession—and ultimately dies.

4. Keeping in Touch With Jesus

Human beings have a wonderful capacity to adjust. My first few days in the military caused me and my fellow draftees enormous stress. After shaving our heads, they gave us our uniforms. My pants reached to the middle of my shins and sported a big dark oil stain right in front. The shoes had space to rent out, and my shirt was too small to allow me to button it. For about 10 days the older soldiers had fun at our expense. We looked and felt like an army of scarecrows. The food, the beds, the discipline, the intimidations, and the most ridiculous orders barked constantly at us made me wonder if I would survive it. Eighteen months later, about one week before discharge, we dreaded the approaching day. A strong camaraderie had developed among us, and we hated to leave one another. In fact, we were ready to die for one another. Back at home it took several weeks to adjust to home cooking, to down-feathered covers, and to the freedom of planning our own lives. Whether it be in prisons or concentration camps, enduring the atrocities of war—in all such circumstances we learn to survive. What a blessing!

Today's lesson with the woman, however, shows us how this ability to adjust can, on the other hand, hurt our discipleship. Sometimes I have thought how wonderful it would be if I could trail Jesus as His disciples did for just a day. Such a privilege would be of incredible benefit to me. Following Jesus for one entire day! Maybe longer! Two or three days! Yet I also recognize that the awe and novelty would soon wear off because of our incredible capacity to adjust, to become used to any extraordinary situation or person. It is true that miracles would always surprise me, but I wonder if after many such experiences I would come to expect them and ultimately take them for granted. And that is a very dangerous situation to be in.

I hear Peter and the other disciples telling Him, "Master, the multitude presses around you, and of course we all touch you all the time, so what is the big deal now?" I can understand. No one can remain excited all the time. The disciples had to do the everyday business of living with, and around, Jesus. Yet I wish that you and I would never come to the point where all of our " touching" would be only casual. I hope that Jesus remains extraordinary for us all the time.

5. LESSON ABOUT CONFESSION

Perhaps the most beautiful moment of this story occurs when the woman realizes that her pain has vanished. If only she could have enjoyed the ecstasy for a while. Why did Jesus have to ask His question so quickly?

So as we watch her come forward we almost feel embarrassed at her fear and trembling and need to confess. Why did she not simply say, "Master, I did it. I'm sorry if that's against the rules. I will do whatever You ask me, but please let me remain whole."

But we cannot dismiss her response by simply ascribing it to her temperament or culture. We suspect some lessons lurk here. First, from the perspective of the woman, several thoughts dash through her mind. She *is* unclean at least until pronounced clean. Healthy, but still ceremonially unclean. Jesus is engaged in a ministry that requires Him to mingle, touch, and be touched. Her action rendered Him unclean, and yes, she prevented Him from moving about until evening lest the people believe that her uncleanliness will spread. How is He going to help Jairus's daughter and many others if He cannot touch them? The day is still young. Wasn't she being selfish by not taking all these factors into account *before* touching Him?

So she had no choice now. What she did was evidently serious enough for Jesus to delay helping Jairus's daughter, so she must be as courageous to confess as she was when she decided to act. This is discipleship. No fudging of the facts, no expecting forgiveness as something automatic because Jesus loves the sinners. It is a matter of honesty with one's self. She might have heard that Scripture does not teach automatic, mechanical, self-regulating forgiveness. Perhaps Proverbs 28:13 came to her mind: "He who conceals his transgressions will not prosper, but he who confesses and forsakes them will obtain mercy."

But Jesus may have His own reasons for exposing the woman and her act. First, He holds her up before us and the crowd as a model and example of tenacity that we should imitate. Despite many years of loneliness and many setbacks she had not given up hope. He is also telling us, His disciples, to protect the marginalized. "Go in peace," He says to her. No one should bother her, scold or harm her, or treat her as though she is still unclean and sick. Her religious community must remember this and involve her talents in service to others. As a result the woman's secret must become public.

As she speaks, no one moves or whispers behind her back. No one snickers. In amazement we listen to Jesus declaring her whole. This is it—no second opinion needed.

MEANING OF DISCIPLESHIP

So little, if anything, has changed since that day in Galilee. We still have the marginalized and rejects roaming our streets. They may be the druggies, drunkards, and mentally disabled, or the maimed and homeless from the wars in Kosovo, Bosnia, or Rwanda. We do not call them untouchables today. Once we referred to them as invalids, which literally means the nonvalid, the not-worth-much people. So we softened it a bit first to handicapped, and then to physically or mentally challenged. Out of sensitivity, you know. Today we may build for them legally required access ramps and legally required elevators. At least we send them help and pray for them. No such thing existed in Jesus' time.

What is the extent of discipleship today? Would Jesus be content with our legally required ramps and elevators? Would they be sufficient to provide complete healing of body and soul to lead people to Him? How would we deal with those who are not important in our neighborhoods if Jesus should walk our streets now and lead our efforts to minister to them?

First, I think He would involve us in unpopular tasks; in the projects that have not the slightest chance to hit the front pages or the TV screens. He would ask us to make regular visits to those in prison or with AIDS. Jesus would want us to care for the elderly, the forgotten men and women whose heroism remains hidden. Can't you see Him inspire all those nameless ones who for years watch after the needy students, the youth of our schools who visit the shut-ins on Sabbath afternoons, the anonymous sponsors who cannot give more than $10 a year, the secretaries and support personnel, the homemakers? They are the ones He would consider His modern disciples. Christ would tell them, "Your Father who sees in secret will reward you" (Matt. 6:4, 6). *Discipleship today means loyalty to those who need us, perseverance in lowly places of labor, and faithfulness without recognition.*

Second, Jesus' concern would quickly turn to the "clean" people among us: the elders, the deacons, the presidents, the chairmen, the directors, the superintendents, the front-pagers—those of us who have to come at night to see Him, because in daylight we seek to be seen with the big shots. He would urge us to experience the new birth. Perhaps He would ask us to lower our cholesterol and blood pressure simply by abandoning our drive for upward mobility. God summons us to be the followers of the Master who healed those that society had written off and learn to share His compassion and desire to make others happy.

Too often, though, we grab for ourselves the prominent places around Him. Modern "untouchables" cannot touch Jesus because the "touchables" (those not spiritually touched by Him anymore) keep them away. In order to reach them, Jesus has to go out of His way to make Himself reachable. *Discipleship today means freedom from rivalry, and freedom for the selfless promotion of the humble.*

Third, He would lead us to open the doors of our hearts and lives to unpleasant people. Secluded and individualistic Christianity contradicts everything He stands for. Jesus never searched for body-guards or clean and pale saints to shield Him from contact with the unclean. Our standards of behavior need face no danger just because we show interest in someone who lives dangerously. Jesus can make our convictions and commitments to Him secure if we reach out to save even the most hopeless cases. He will become the bridge between "us" and "them" so we can see from close range the needs and hopes hidden behind the rags of unworthiness, filth, and stench. *Discipleship today means taking risks outside of our comfort zone in order to expose Jesus to their touch.*

Fourth, still under the shock of seeing Jesus unreachable, the woman in amazement notices Him veer in her direction. *He noticed me,* she must have thought. *For 12 years no one walked purposefully toward me. On the contrary, everybody who could, avoided me. Am I really worth the trouble the Master is going through?*

Again, nothing has changed in the area of basic human needs. Today Jesus wants us to remember that we tell others of their worth by how far we are ready to go in serving them, by how much time we carve out just for them, by how much difference in lifestyle we can tolerate without offending or being offended.

A family moved in three houses down the street. They belonged to another denomination. Within the first two weeks my wife went to meet them and give them a loaf of my homemade bread. "We thought no one would speak to us or welcome us," the wife said, "because we worship differently than most of you and because my husband smokes."

Discipleship means inviting people of other persuasions a bit closer, so we can share Jesus together.

Finally, the Master would counsel us to stay close to the newly converted Christians for our benefit. The longer we have been in the church, the more sensitive we should become to the privileges of discipleship. But too often we have become too sophisticated to notice the good things around us. As a large family, we hear stuff, and share stuff, and become angry about so much stuff that we become too overstuffed to see anything beyond the stuff. Our own healing did not happen in one moment. If only we would befriend those who are still touched by our pastor's sermon, those who admire Sister Rose or Brother Bill and whose childlike faith still stops Jesus in His tracks. It would rejuvenate us. Just one caution though: don't share the bad stuff with them. *Discipleship today means willful ignorance of the dark tales circulating about us and a renewed childlike trust in our fellow Christians.*

CHAPTER 9

The Storm

"LOOK, MA, NO HANDS!"

The development of certain skills indicates to every child that without a shadow of a doubt he or she is growing up. The ability to ride a bike is one of them, and for boys it is a very important one. I remember when we went to the store to buy a bike for our firstborn. Just the expression on his face made all the expense affordable.

That afternoon I took Andrej alone to a quiet street for his first lesson. "Simply look up and ahead of you. No, you don't need to watch your feet. Pedal forward, son! That's the way! I told you, you can do it!" And he did. One year later Adam, our younger son, learned it as well. The final exam, though, happened when they could ride with no hands—and show it to their mom. And, as tradition would want it, when Ma watches, some stupid stone flips the front wheel, and yes, we witnessed one of the greatest falls of destiny.

• • •

Finally it is late afternoon. The extremely exhausting day is almost over. Jesus has lectured for several hours, fed the crowd of 5,000, and resisted an attempt at making Him a king. Now He desires to be alone. "Immediately he made his disciples get into the boat and go before him to the other side, to Bethsaida, while he dismissed the crowd. And after he had taken leave of them, he went up on the mountain to pray. And when evening came, the boat was out on the sea, and he was alone on the land" (Mark 6:45-47). Just then, as happens frequently on the lake, a strong wind picks up as dense masses of air suddenly and violently avalanche down the hillsides to the lake surface, which is nearly 700 feet below sea level. The wind begins to churn the water. Such a storm can develop quickly even on a clear day. Jesus watches from the shore as the disciples strain at the oars, trying to make headway against the powerful wind.

After some time He decides to join the boat and give them a hand. But how? Well, the boat is already some distance out on the lake. Imagine the shivers along their spine as the disciples, already in distress, see someone walk by on the top of the water (verse 48). Terrified, the men screamed from fear, thinking it was a ghost. "But immediately he spoke to them, saying, 'Take heart, it is I; have no fear'" (Matt. 14:27).

Then the ever-impulsive Peter shouts over the wind, "Lord, if it is You, bid me come to You on the water." If You can walk on it, how about me? So Jesus calls back, "Come." Peter, forgetting the storm, puts one foot out, then the other, and the water molecules hold together as never before, so he too can walk all the way to Jesus. That is, almost. Unfortunately, the marvelous experience lasts only too short a time. Peter knows what water is. More than once he has literally missed the boat and fallen into it. He knows how deep and merciless the lake can be in such storms. Would it not have been better to stay in the boat with the others than to be out in the open with nothing solid under his feet?

The disciples, not knowing how Peter feels, must have been tempted to try it themselves. I wonder if anyone (Judas, perhaps), seeing how Peter and Jesus defied the laws of nature, now thought of what walking on water could mean for professional fishers. They would no longer need boats or have to fear drowning. You could throw your gear over the shoulder, go for a stroll on the sea wherever you wished, then pull the net full of fish back to the shore. Judas could form a "Water-Walker's Fishing Co." and no one could compete with their method of catching fish.

But just then they saw their comrade sinking and calling for help. "Lord, save me." Jesus immediately reached out, and pulling Peter to

Himself, said softly, "'O man of little faith, why did you doubt?' And when they got into the boat, the wind ceased. And those in the boat worshiped him, saying, 'Truly you are the Son of God'" (verses 28-33).

LESSONS OF DISCIPLESHIP

To be with Jesus, especially in the same boat with Him, can be a fun experience. Discipleship is not just hard work. It does not concentrate only on serious stuff—sins and evil consequences—and it is not always solemn. Christians have often focused their preaching and thinking on the evils and tragedies around them, imagining the pain that humans cause their heavenly Father when they sin. To be sure, flippancy and carelessness in mood and behavior are never prudent, and playfulness with sin always spells tragedy. But today we observe in this storm a lighter side of Christianity, a more innocent, candid, and simple way to relate to Jesus. We treat Him as our Master, and He relates to us as friends.

1. LESSON OF TEMPERANCE

"Miroslav, when was the last time you took your weekly day off?" P. F. Lemon, my conference president, asked me one Monday morning.

"Well, I really do not have time for that right now, Elder. My Bible studies, visitations, and It Is Written requests keep me busy."

"Listen to me, young man. Why don't you cancel your appointments for this week, pick up your little family, head south to Vermont, find a cabin, and return on Sunday. We in the office will take care of your church for this Sabbath. If you cannot take a weekly day off, take two days bi-weekly. You need rest, and your family and your church need you rested."

Today Jesus teaches us temperance in work. Killing ourselves as we work for His sake is not a sacrifice that pleases Him. Damaging our health through excessive stress and strain can lead to transgression of the sixth commandment. True, sometimes we may have to put forth extra effort, but not constantly. While the slave owners loved their workaholic slaves, Jesus is not a slave owner. As for Himself, He knew when He needed to be alone, so He took the necessary steps to make it possible. He dismissed the crowd of 5,000 that He had fed and that apparently intended to linger around for breakfast too.

Jesus wanted people to learn respect for His own needs. He would allow nothing to cheat Him out of His own private time off or interfere with His daily communion with His Father. Unfortunately, even His closest followers were not always willing to let Him be by Himself, so He "made the disciples get into the boat and go before him to the other side" (Matt. 14:22). Ever since the creation of our world He has been trying to teach us that regular rest is an integral part of work.

His concern for rest extends to His disciples as well. Not long before, the disciples had returned from their own mission to the nearby towns and villages. They came back excited about the experiences they had had teaching, healing, and casting out demons. "And he said to them, 'Come away by yourselves to a lonely place, and rest a while.' For many were coming and going, and they had no leisure even to eat" (Mark 6:31). It is good to remember that Christians always work first and foremost for a sensitive and caring Master.

2. Jesus, a Good Sport

Now the storm is raging, putting the lives of the disciples in immediate danger. Jesus comes to their rescue. Peter knows from his long experience on the lake that the boat is still the safest place to be. Why, then, is he willing to venture out on the water? Despite the fact that he and the others are facing death, does he still have some taste for adventure, still have a streak of curiosity? Or is it an incurable desire to show off, to be first again? Whatever the reason, Peter knows who Jesus is, what kind of Person He is, and what sort of things are OK in His presence. If this really is Jesus, He might, just might, let Peter walk on the water.

So what kind of Person is the Jesus that Peter knows?

In this incident we discover Him to be a good sport. Jesus bore such titles as the Son of man, the Son of God, and the Messiah. The Master could speak of God as His Father, and He performed miracles not for show but for the good of others. He was the Teacher, and

His disciples were just that—pupils. Many responsibilities, duties, and prerogatives belonged only to Him. Thus Jesus could easily have said, "Peter, you stay right there until I come. Do not rock the boat now! The best thing you can do now is *nothing!*"

But Jesus loves our humanness, including the genuine and natural humanness of Peter. Although He knows that the disciple is not ready yet for the kind of experience he seeks, instead of barring him, Jesus says "Come." Try it. Even two steps made by faith can impress this man so he will never lose the taste for it. Every power in His possession Jesus gladly shares with His disciples. Some days earlier they had told Him how it felt to see the sick, the demoniacs, and the hopeless regain their health and sanity again. I would not be surprised if even Judas received from this selfless Master the same abilities.

In that one word, "Come," it is as if Jesus is saying: "Come, Peter. Walk through the storm. Brave the waves in a way you never did before. Kick the foam of the raging sea, just as you kicked the dust with your childhood feet. Come. You will get wet, you will get frightened, but I can pull you out. You can do all things through My strength."

3. LESSON OF KINDNESS

So Peter did begin his trek across the storm-tossed lake, and now the other disciples watched two "ghosts" walk on the waves. Jesus never boasts, glorifies Himself, or expects to be flattered. But Peter is a different story. He was already a difficult person to live with. Now what will he be like after walking on water? For who knows how long he will probably brag about his experience, and his friends will have to listen and acknowledge what a great adventure he had. Perhaps they will wish that they had had the guts to do it too.

After several steps, just at the instant when the feeling "Look, Ma, no hands" begins to emerge, a large wave rushes between him and Jesus. The water on the surface of the lake can hold the weight of a person. It's somewhat firm. If the wave were just a stationary rock, he could climb over it. But this watery "rock" hurtles toward him. What if it remains hard when it hits him? Peter wants to see the reaction of his comrades, and in that moment he loses sight of the

Master. The water molecules start behaving normally again. Peter's heart sinks, and his body follows.

"But while the billows talk with death, Peter lifts his eyes from the angry waters, and fixing them upon Jesus, cries, 'Lord save me'"*(The Desire of Ages,* p. 381). "You, Jesus, only You can save me now. It is all over with now. But You, Jesus, You do not sink. The storms and the depths of our sinful world dare not harm You. You are the only one on this globe who can hold me up. Please, would You?"

What happens now is an enormous lesson to us all. "Jesus immediately reached out his hand and caught him, saying to him, 'O man of little faith, why did you doubt?'" (Matt. 14:31). Some of us, in Jesus' place, possessing His powers, would perhaps wait until Peter got a bit soaked. Or if we saved him immediately, he would have to pay! We would take him to the boat while teasing him, enjoying a good hearty laugh at his expense. And probably Peter wouldn't mind.

But Jesus is not that way. He is kind with Peter, even when He used the experience to reinforce a lesson about doubt and faith. We like following this Master, because He will forgive us even if we make fools of ourselves in His company.

4. Lesson of Direction

It is not so strange that my son insisted on looking down at his feet when he began to learn to ride a bike. We all know that our eyes perceive danger more quickly than any other sense. We see at the speed of light (186,000 miles per second) while we hear at the speed of sound (about 1,100 feet per second). We also know that we must watch in the direction we are heading, and that if we drive, we had better be aware of what is going on in every direction. Imagine how hard it is for a blind person to navigate in an unknown environment. Think how foolish it would be to drive through an intersection without looking, to operate machinery without watching, to tend to your face or hair without a mirror, to hear a gunshot and not try to see where the danger comes from. Wherever the action is, that's where our eyes go instinctively.

Not so with bike riding. We must not look where the action is, or we will lose our balance. The same thing applies to following

Jesus. Do you think it would not be normal for Peter to see the waves, to hear the storm, and to know that the boat may sink any moment, and not to look where the action is? I know I would do the same. Why should I look at Jesus when He is not the trouble-maker or not in danger? Because otherwise I will lose my balance. My life will go in the direction my eyes look. Just as my son had to shift his attention away from his feet and concentrate on the direction he was going, so the disciples must turn away from the waves and focus on Jesus, both the author and the goal of their life. Wherever Jesus is, that's forward, that's the right way, that's where our next step should be. Any other direction will only lead us astray.

5. In the Same Boat With Jesus

Back in the boat we watch and listen. Jesus is quiet, as are Peter and the other disciples, and also the sea. No more winds whip the waves into a froth, and no more danger threatens the little vessel. I imagine Peter pondering and reliving every second again, and his friends rowing quietly as if they had all lost their power of speech. Only a short time ago they had insisted on making Him their king. The well-fed crowd would have completely supported Him. All He needed to do was to accept the offer, and no one could have stood in His way. Since then the disciples had seen that even the winds and the waves obeyed Him. But now they felt a bit foolish for even thinking He would need their help.

What they have learned is that Jesus also keeps His eyes away from where the action is. He too looks beyond the immediate context. His Father is His forward direction, where the eternal solution awaits for Peter and the rest of humanity. No true and lasting peace exists inside or outside of the boat, unless it is where His Father wants Him to be. And He is not embarrassed to admit that His eyes are riveted elsewhere—that He does not do what the circumstances dictate nor what He wants. In John 5:19 Jesus says to His critics: "The Son can do nothing of his own accord, but only what he sees the Father doing; for whatever he does, that the Son does likewise."

As long as they ride in the same boat with Jesus, the disciples discover that they are not at the mercy of their trials and fears, because

He is in charge. No one can mock or hurt them as long as He is there. So whatever happens now, Peter can sit quietly for the rest of the journey. In a very true sense, he can be a child again. He can try new things, fail, and begin again. Nowhere is he so fully accepted, nor is anyone so genuinely willing to give him the opportunity to spill out whatever fancy comes to his mind, as with Jesus. And what is more, Jesus still gives him the full respect accorded to an adult.

MEANING OF DISCIPLESHIP

Christians should be happy people. The storm on the lake reveals several reasons that the life of discipleship is the only genuine existence there is even today.

First, when we work for Jesus we will not be as prone to stress. But when I say "work for Jesus," I do not mean just evangelism, Bible studies, or involvement in our local church, as good and valuable as such things are. Rather, when we go to our place of labor—whether it be kitchen, factory, office, field, or church—and we have as our goal to do and be today what we know is in harmony with Jesus' way and lifestyle, that's when our fears and worries will diminish to a minimum. As others see that we do not intend to hurt anyone and that our motives are Christlike, the people around us will not hesitate to befriend us. They will trust us and enjoy our company. In addition, when we act as we know Jesus would, we reduce the likelihood of our actions leading to bad consequences, thus making us more confident about the future. More important, when we remember that a disciple works for the Master first and the employer second, our sense of responsibility, our accountability, will not change whether the boss watches us or we are alone and without supervision. *Discipleship today means keeping Christlikeness as the main motive and purpose of our life's work.*

Second, the storm teaches us that Jesus' manner of being a boss or a leader is the most caring way to lead. For instance, Jesus' main objective is not quantity of things done. Many face a great temptation to employ or submit to that kind of leadership. We want more shoes made, more fields plowed, more cars repaired, more converts baptized, and we assume that it makes us better workers. Jesus knew that when the disciples returned from their missionary journey they had not met all the people's needs. He saw the continuing eagerness and needs of the men, women, and children who followed them. But Jesus recognized also that overwork can dehumanize the laborers, whether they be involved in evangelism or engineering.

At times we catch ourselves working for praise, for advancement, or for money. Some of us try to bury our disappointment with our kids or the break ups in our other relationships by throwing ourselves into what on the outside appears to be "sacrificial" labor. But money, guilt, or praise make bad, un-Christlike bosses. *Discipleship today means keeping Jesus at the helm of our enterprises and ventures. His presence may not be the most profitable or the most reputable option from a human perspective, but disciples are unique people who place the kingdom of God at the top of their scale of values.*

Third, the itinerary Jesus follows does not avoid all the storms and threats to our lives. His disciples throughout the ages have frequently faced serious danger while obeying His will. That night, when the twelve set out to cross the lake, they acted on their Master's orders, yet He did not prevent the storm, and the waves almost submerged them all. Yet with Jesus in our boat—in our life—we make it through our storms, whether they be losses (of job, spouse, health, etc.) or challenges, with His help. No longer alone, we find ourselves in the company of the real Master of the universe. Instead of sinking according to the laws of nature, we will walk on the top of the waves that would otherwise swallow us. Jesus has many often-unexpected ways of handling our problems. He can even enable us to say or do or bear or see what normally we could never manage alone.

Just knowing that He is really our traveling companion, because we answered His call to follow Him, will turn our gaze beyond our sickness to how He will use that sickness, from our loss to how He will handle our pain, or from our wounds to how He will heal us. *Discipleship today means having courage when others despair. We have access to our Master's resources when our human wisdom cries out for help.*

Fourth, we must revisit the boat after the storm. Peter's glory turned so quickly to gloom. He sits, shaking from both fear and cold, not daring to look up for shame. (The boat does not offer much privacy.) The once-boastful disciple now fully expects to be the object of fun and mockery. So often that is what happens when we try some unusual experiment with good intentions, only to have our project fail. "Many would like to have written, but few actually dare" has been attributed to Winston Churchill. To take time and energy, to expose your thinking to others, and then, when you have made the investment, to receive a rejection slip—that is a hard thing to endure!

The amazing fact is, though, that no one said a word or snickered Peter's way. It was not because they had all been converted that night. Rather, "when they got into the boat, the wind ceased. And those in the boat worshiped him, saying 'Truly you are the Son of God'" (Matt. 14:32, 33).

One wonders how much more pleasant and restful our lives could be if we all would worship our Lord, His greatness and success, whenever we have to face up to failure. Perhaps it is election time in the local church and the list of officers does not contain our names; a low test score; being passed over for a job; or an evangelistic campaign that brought not even one baptism. When someone feels wet, shivering, cold, and totally exposed, what can we do to help? I have made enough public blunders in speaking or singing that I make it a habit to tell others that nothing we do is primarily for people. God is our boss always. In the church we sing to or praise Him. He hears us the way we want to sing, not the way we actually do. And that is true for any service of love we engage in. Jesus loved Peter's walk. It was just tremendous. Only a bit more faith, and he will get it. *Discipleship today means that when we regard our service to others as a performance for God, we will seek only His appreciation.*

CHAPTER 10

The Kiss

FAILING IN THE SCHOOL OF JESUS

We must fast-forward to the last week of the three and a half years of Jesus' instructional ministry. The disciples will soon face the most formidable final exam of their life, and not all will pass. One of them will fail miserably, while another will have to do some major remedial work. The best Teacher the world has ever known could not guarantee graduation for everybody.

It actually all started at the very beginning of Jesus' ministry. He had already selected most of His disciples, and they followed Him about regularly. Many of them had come from a humble background, mostly fishers or tradespeople. The Master Himself held no rabbinical credentials, and some of the disciples wished that at least one person from the upper classes would join the group. But how do you make such a lifestyle attractive to someone used to comfort and the service of others?

In Capernaum one day "a scribe came up and said to him, 'Teacher, I will follow you wherever you go'" (Matt. 8:19). The disciples thought he was an answer to prayer. But Jesus curiously did not act as excited as they did. "Foxes have holes," He replied, "and birds of the air have nests; but the Son of man has nowhere to lay his head" (verse 20). Puzzled and disappointed with such a lack of welcome, the disciples watched and hoped that Judas would stay anyway.

It was an unusual beginning. Instead of being handpicked by the

Master, Judas requests to join, and in the absence of a definite rejection, he stays. Could it be that Jesus knew his unusual end and so He hesitated without rejecting him outright? But Judas stayed because he loved Jesus, His ministry, and His teachings. The man himself recognized the need for a change in his character that only Jesus could give him. Judas arrived with the best of intentions.

We watch him next at the dinner given in honor of Jesus by Simon the Pharisee. Throughout the more than three years that follow we do not notice Judas in any particular way. He is a leader who works from within, who makes plans and exerts his influence in a quiet, almost subtle way. It is now just two days before the Passover and the Feast of Unleavened Bread. During the meal at Simon's home someone opens a flask of expensive perfumed oil and pours out its contents lavishly, almost wastefully, on Jesus' feet. Being the financial officer of the School of Jesus (John 13:29) and astute and informed about the commercial trends of the day, Judas objects. " 'Why was this ointment not sold for three hundred denarii and given to the poor?' This he said, not because he cared for the poor but because he was a thief, and as he had the money box he used to take what was put into it. Jesus said, 'Let her alone, let her keep it for the day of my burial. The poor you always have with you, but you do not always have me' " (John 12:5-8).

When he hears Jesus' words something snaps in Judas's mind. Such fiscal irresponsibility is just too much for him. A Messiah who would lead His people out of political, social, economic, and financial misery must be an example of frugality. Jesus' version of discipleship is bad business at best—definitely a money-losing venture. Besides, Jesus of late acts too melancholy. He constantly talks about suffering, burial, depression, and departure. Is He a fraud? Lacking willpower to lead, He is too immersed in His dreams. What He needs is a reality check.

Before anybody else leaves, Judas departs Simon's home in Bethany and runs to Jerusalem to the chief priests with a plan he has in mind. He knows something definite will happen this time around, and he must be on the winning side. First he will offer to deliver Jesus into the hands of the priests, but for a price paid in silver or gold. Once that happens, he will watch Jesus free Himself. For the sake of the people He will have to take charge and lead. The crowds will turn against the national leaders. The trouble until now has been that no one dared to force Jesus to face the realities of the political world. Everyone just waits for Him to take the first step, and by nature He is too conscientious a man.

It is only pure coincidence that the 30 pieces of silver happen to be the traditional price of a slave. Besides, Jesus is always around. No one really needs to help His enemies find Him. The priests will accept Judas's help only because it will look like a betrayal—as if one of His closest disciples cannot stand Him anymore. But God, Judas reasons, knows his heart. The Lord knows how much he loves and respects Jesus. He will judge Judas according to his heart, not according to his deeds.

Next we find Judas with the other disciples, eating their Passover meal. Jesus washes their feet. Some disciples object, but Judas probably perceives it to be a smart move on the Master's part to show Himself humble just before His coronation. Everything Judas sees Jesus do, or hears Him say, he interprets according to his own preconceived ideas.

Yet this proves to be the most annoying evening for Judas ever. He had never understood what Jesus meant about a year ago when He had said, "Did I not choose you, the twelve, and one of you is a devil?" (John 6:70). But that statement is mild compared with things that Judas has to face now. First, Jesus is again in the throes of another of His melancholy moods, except this time it is much stronger. He openly speaks about crucifixion, about His death. His ramblings visibly disturb the disciples, but Judas winks at them, implying, "Do not pay too much attention to this. It will pass; you'll see."

Then Jesus makes Judas a bit more uncomfortable. He says that a servant is not greater than his master, nor is the messenger greater than the one who sends him. A simple statement of truth, but what He means is that one of those who eats at the table—a disciple—will strike against Him, the Master (John 13:16-18). Judas is restless. *Could Jesus possibly know? But how? Who would have told Him?*

Jesus does not let up on the pressure. "Truly, truly, I say to you, one of you will betray me" (verse 21). *Well, He knows! The best thing to do now is to lie low.* Agitated, the disciples all question who the traitor is, so Judas plays the role of an innocent friend. But Peter cannot stand such tensions. He has to know. It is not for nothing that he carries his sword. Perhaps he can stop the rascal cold in his steps. Maybe he can get Jesus to reveal who it is. The Master always treats John, the youngest disciple, with particular care. Perhaps John can help now. At Peter's urging John asks Jesus, "Lord, who is it?"

Judas waits with fear. Why don't Peter and John mind their own business? "Jesus answered, 'It is he to whom I shall give this morsel when I have dipped it.' So when he had dipped the morsel, he gave it to Judas, the son of Simon Iscariot" (verses 26, 27).

Do you see all the eyes following that morsel from the plate to the cup with wine, from the cup up and to the side where Judas sits (the other side of the table relaxes a bit), and then straight to Judas's mouth? The Gospel of Matthew records one more step Jesus takes in spelling out how serious the act of betrayal is. No amount of rationalization will help. "The Son of man goes as it is written of him, but woe to that man by whom the Son of man is betrayed! It would have been better for that man if he had not been born." To this, Judas, faking anxiety, asks, " 'Is it I, Master?' He said to him, 'You have said so' " (Matt. 26:25).

Like a guided missile that strikes its target, the morsel lands where it belongs, but it does not explode. Not yet. Their admiration of Judas blinds them. Judas can do nothing wrong in their eyes. *He is such a nice guy.* In addition, it is the custom for intimate friends to share food with each other. Jesus is showing Judas that He still loves Him—that it is not too late even now.

"Then after the morsel, Satan entered into him. Jesus said to him, 'What you are going to do, do quickly.' Now no one at the table knew why he said this to him. Some thought that, because Judas had the money box, Jesus was telling him, 'Buy what we need for the feast'; or, that he should give something to the poor. So, after receiving the morsel, he immediately went out; and it was night" (John 13:27-30).

Even the demonstration of love through the offering of food as well as Jesus' appeals to his conscience could not sway Judas from his plan. After that sudden exit, he never again rejoins the company of the disciples. He might have thought, *Jesus will turn the other disciples against me, and what then of my silver?* When we find him the next time, it is in the Garden of Gethsemane on a most disgraceful errand. As Jesus finishes His agonizing prayer and sees the disciples asleep, He finds to His dismay one who is not slumbering with them. Judas is wide awake. "And he came up to Jesus at once and said, 'Hail, Master!' And he kissed him" (Matt. 26:49). "But Jesus said to him, 'Judas, would you betray the Son of man with a kiss?'" (Luke 22:48).

The kiss. A lofty expression of respect, affection, and love becomes a mask that hides the most hideous of acts: the treachery. To betray me would be an insult, but to betray Jesus, whose goodness and sinless love cannot be surpassed—and to do it to Him face-to-face—that qualifies as the most degrading crime of all human history. And Judas could not stand the tremendous burden of guilt. Imagine him watching what happens to Jesus. After the Temple police fell to the ground as if dead, He could have walked away, avoiding their stunned bodies while whistling a happy tune. But to Judas's dismay, Jesus stays there. After they tied Him up, He could have broken those ropes in no time, as Samson did, but Jesus doesn't even try. After they led Him to the high priest's house, Judas thought that He would stun everybody here, in the very residence of His archenemy—but nothing happens. After the mocking, beating, and spitting have lasted too long, even then Jesus bears it calmly, with no reaction at all.

But in the morning, when Caiaphas and other priests condemn Jesus to death and lead Him away to Pilate, Judas's hopes and dreams collapse around him. To others, Jesus was just one of the wannabe messiahs, while to the disciples He had become an incomprehensible Saviour. But Judas sees Him suddenly as a Lamb led helplessly to the slaughter. All at once the prophecies about the need for His suffering and death become as clear as day. But it is too late for Judas. He cannot force himself to ask for forgiveness, cannot see Jesus, the Lamb, as his substitute. A scream interrupts the gruesome scene. "'I have sinned in betraying innocent blood!' They said, 'What is that to us? See to it yourself.' And throwing down the pieces of silver in the temple, he departed; and he went and hanged himself" (Matt. 27:4, 5).

LESSONS OF DISCIPLESHIP

When disciples join Jesus, their lives become closely intertwined with Him and one another. His school is not just an institution; His discipleship is not just a curriculum of theoretical instruction. In the same way, Christianity is not a system of habits and practices carefully defined and supervised by church hierarchy. Rather, discipleship of Christ is the definition of a life that has for its goal and purpose outliving death. The lessons from Judas's tragedy illustrate this point vividly.

1. LESSON ABOUT INTENTIONS

Intentions are important drives that orient and inform our will to act. For example, we want to help a person who has just been injured by a hit-and-run driver. Our intentions are pure and good. Have we not learned from the story of the good Samaritan to help injured people? Yet in spite of our good intentions, we could aggravate the injury a hundredfold if we so much as move the victim in the wrong way. This example tells us that good intentions cannot guarantee the goodness of the outcome of our actions. They cannot, for example, prevent dislocated or shattered vertebrae from permanently damaging the spinal cord and causing paralysis if we move the victim in the wrong way. Our intentions, besides being good, must be correctly informed.

This is where Judas teaches us a lesson. His mind remains fixed on what he wants to accomplish and how he thinks it should be done. But Judas ignores too many facets of Jesus' complex mission even to dream himself qualified to assume the role of His agent, deciding when and what Jesus should do and how He should do it. The goodness of his intentions is too temporal, too limited, too earthly. He refuses to see what Nicodemus finally understood—that spiritual things must be understood and acted upon in spiritual ways. Judas never grasped the fact that spiritual things must have priority over temporal concerns. Jesus is not just a political, economic, social, and military Saviour, leaving the cause of all evils—human sin—untouched. No, He is first of all the Saviour *from* sin, preparing His followers for a kingdom that will have forever eradicated political, economic, and social evils. He first eliminates the cause of all evil and only then sets up His kingdom.

Moreover, intentions may have a crippling effect on our will. During my childhood I often heard the dictum "The path to hell is paved with good intentions." Without a doubt, Jesus touched Judas's heart many times and in different ways. Judas probably thought it would be good someday to sit down and open his heart and mind to Jesus, and perhaps to clarify things between them. Jesus certainly gave him ample opportunities to do just that during the last week of their walk together. But the disciple never got around to doing it. Intentions, when informed and good, must be acted upon—otherwise they have no impact on our lives.

2. Lesson About Success/Failure

For a long time I did not understand the true nature of discipleship and its essential difference from our present-day educational experience. But Judas's case teaches us that learning from Jesus involves more than memorizing information, understanding theological concepts, or explaining or convincing others of the truth of Christianity. Discipleship is the way we live that information—the way our knowledge of truth affects our thinking, our organization of priorities, and our relationship with ourselves and others. It is not what we know, what we can do, or what we have, but *who we are.* Our Master seeks to accomplish a total change of our worldview, so that we can see what He sees and like what He likes while still retaining our individuality.

This kind of curriculum, and the objective it seeks to achieve, has infinitely more far-reaching impact on human life than conventional schooling. God does not ask the disciple to be a miniature Jesus, controlled by a full-size Jesus through some kind of remote control. What really happens is that we come to live life much more intensely and aware. At every step, facing every decision, Christ's followers learn to pay full attention to the alternatives involved in their choice, and because of their vital connection with the divine perspective, subjective human impulses play a lesser role. Life's turning points are now less confusing and its general direction more explicit.

Let me illustrate. Judas thought he had a clear vision of both who he was and who Jesus was. On that basis he conceived a definite kind of kingdom of heaven, a vision that directed his ambition and his actions. But he was wrong—very wrong. Although he waited for the arrival of God's kingdom, he unknowingly acted according to the principles of the kingdom of darkness. As in much conventional learning, he opted to keep his knowledge of the gospel on a theoretical level, while his actions followed impulses totally unaffected by that gospel.

Now, the advantage Judas had in being Christ's disciple was that Jesus gave him consistent feedback for every move, tendency, or decision he faced. At a spiritual crossroad, if Judas gave a left blinker signal, Jesus did not reach out to correct Judas's move. Instead He told Judas where he would wind up if he did turn to the left. This kind of rapport with the Master is what a life of discipleship is all about, and it is a far cry from theoretical know-how. The grades we receive in the school of Jesus are not "pass/fail," but something like "hot/lukewarm/cold" (Rev. 3:15, 16). They do not refer to what we know, but rather to what the state of our soul is—where we are in reference to heaven or how our behavior, thinking, desires, and ambitions are in tune with the etiquette of the heavenly kingdom.

3. LESSON ABOUT THE POINT OF NO RETURN

Can you see the point of no return in Judas's experience? For years he insisted on his own way, and Jesus respected his choices. Judas was physically present and involved in Jesus' programs and various projects, but his heart and mind always headed in his own uncommitted direction. On the outside, nothing appeared to alarm his colleagues or alert them to the need to minister to him. It was a definite case of a double life. On one occasion, during the Sermon on the Mount, Jesus declared: "No one can serve two masters; for either he will hate the one and love the other, or he will be devoted to the one and despise the other. You cannot serve God and mammon" (Matt. 6:24). Judging by later events, it is likely that Judas listened to Jesus' sermon. Mentally he could not challenge the statement's truthfulness, and possibly he promised himself that he would commit himself to just one master.

Ultimately he did, but it was the wrong one.

All this continued in secret until that evening of the Passover supper, when the forces of evil fought the final battle against the Master's efforts to save Judas. The words of Jesus "What you are going to do, do quickly" (John 13:27) have an unmistakable ring of finality. Judas is heading for ruin, and Jesus told him so. It is as if Jesus were saying, "If you really think your design for saving the world is better and you insist on following it against all warnings, then let it be. I will not swerve from My course, but I certainly wish you would from yours. Why are you so much more committed to mammon than to Me? No, it did not begin like this, remember? You never intended that our relationship end in this manner. But now, where you go I cannot go. Our paths will openly diverge from this moment on." This time Jesus' efforts failed. The free human will can always resist Jesus. Judas went out alone, "and it was night" (verse 30).

4. Lesson About Appearances

Each individual human being is a mystery. Like an impregnable fortress, our mind resists all attempts to violate its private space. Don't you wish sometimes you could pick into your child's thinking, or your spouse's inner world, just so you would know, once and for all, who they really are? But as long as no one can enter this inner sanctum of our being we can still speak of individual freedom, and by the same token we must expect to err in assessing others or in being appraised by them.

The riddle of Judas in the company of the other disciples teaches us the lesson of prudence. During their entire journey together the disciples could not free themselves from his spell. Even as they sat at the feet of the divine Master, they were still vulnerable to evil influences. The great deceiver chose the most prominent, the most promising, and the most gifted man among them in order to undermine Jesus and the future of His mission. Think of the shock when they saw him deliver Jesus, rather than protect Him from the mob of criminals. With consternation they discover who his true friends are. Under the flickering light of the torches they finally recognize the real Judas. An ominous sense of insecurity, suspicion, and mutual mistrust now threatened their fellowship. Could they trust anyone? Who would be the next deserter among them? But most of all, they felt cheated, fooled, and angry. They learned that no one except Jesus deserves the admiration and confidence they gave to this miserable man.

5. LESSON IN LEADERSHIP

Think of the interhuman dynamics that had existed among the disciples for three and a half years. Consider the delicate balance Jesus had to maintain in leading these men while tolerating Judas in their midst. It is not as if Jesus had no other alternatives. He could, as do some leaders today, have marginalized him, slowly eliminating him from planning and consultation sessions and from important assignments. A feeling of being bypassed offers a strong incentive to leave, and Judas, being a proud man, would probably have done so.

Moreover, Jesus could have openly confronted him when the first sum of money disappeared. He could have waited for a perfect situation to arise that Judas could not explain his way out of, and in that case the other disciples would have demanded his dismissal. Financial fraud is a highly sensitive issue to everyone.

Finally, Jesus could have simply forced the disciples to choose whom they would follow. He could have pulled the tares from His patch of garden for the sake of purity. If His disciples are to be the model for His church for centuries to come, characters such as Judas could have no place in His company.

But nothing of the kind happened. We learn that His leadership gives every human being sufficient opportunity and ample time to consider their ways and change. Even though God knows our future and the final outcome is as clear to Him as the present, He makes the rain fall and the sun shine on all in equal proportion. Jesus will not sacrifice people to programs. He did not discard Judas as a piece of trash just because of the disciple's opposition to, and lack of cooperation in, the most magnificent plan of redemption in the history of the universe. The Master was not willing that anyone die, *Judas included*.

6. LESSON ABOUT POLITICS

Politics is everywhere, but politics is not everything. If, because of the frailty and weakness of human nature, we encounter its misuse and abuse all around us, we also sense that unethical political schemes are incompatible with our own calling as disciples. This is the lesson we learn from Jesus' treatment of Judas. It is amazing to see how He kept clear of all types of manipulation, pressure tactics, character assassination, doctoring of evidence, innuendo, and intimidation strategy throughout His time in office. He had no use for such props. His ways challenge the assumption that good ends justify un-Christlike means in any area of life, including the management of His goods. He refuses to let Judas force such menus into His organization—the church. Nor does He lead His disciples on such paths. "My kingship is not of this world," Jesus told Pilate (John 19:36), and His subjects find their pleasure in following His example.

MEANING OF DISCIPLESHIP

We cannot find any more relevant lessons for today than those contained in the tragic biography of Judas. Who cannot occasionally see one's own self in his dilemmas, temptations, and failures?

First, how many times, like Judas, have we, when facing an issue, immediately turned to our human resources for counsel and strength, seeking God's help only when everything else fails? Who among us has had enough patience and fortitude to wait until His time comes and His methods begin to show results? We too come to Jesus with requests, but also with convictions as to what answers we will accept from Him. Judas wanted Jesus to be the Messiah, but on his own terms, just as we want Him to bless us and save us on our terms. The disciple could not take no for an answer, and frankly, we have similar difficulties, don't we? *Discipleship today means keeping our minds open to unusual answers to our prayers and to God's surprising routings for our way home.*

Second, our busy schedules and fast pace give us little opportunity to spend meaningful time with our Master. Time to let down our defenses, to become vulnerable to His Word, and to hear Him tell us about who we really can become. Postponing the needs of our inner life because we worry about food and drink, our living room and garage, and a few titles and degrees we want to attach to our name, is what Judas did—and he lost it all, both his silver and his soul. *Discipleship today means to revise our schedules so that we can have time for a genuine meeting of minds, hearts, emotions, and plans with our Master.*

Third, we too may be prone to value a person by what we see—their external aspects. "I don't remember what he said, but it was interesting, and he's such a nice person." Or "I don't care much about her religion or her lifestyle, but she pleases me well." While we must refrain from judging people, we are also advised to refer to the law and the testimony, and, like the Bereans, search to know where this charming or eloquent person is leading us.

I feel particularily cautious toward the audiocassettes so many people listen to today. Tapes are different than books. Before I buy or read a book, I check the publisher, the author, and the content. The publisher's reputation and quality control by the editors add to the safety of my reading. But even when all seems fine I can still scan a book, check its contents, read the introduction and conclusion, and then decide whether to purchase and read it. I can decide whether to invest my time and expose my mind to that of the author. But a tape does not offer me such a luxury. By the time I feel strange about its content the damage may already be done. *Discipleship in the present information age means carefully screening people and influences before we expose ourselves to them.*

Fourth, prominent people do not automatically deserve to be followed. Is this not the message Paul gives us in 1 Corinthians 1:11-17? Neither Apollos, Cephas, or Paul is anything, he says. Only Christ is. We may prefer certain leaders, speakers, authors, or friends, but we cannot admire them excessively or follow them blindly. No one deserves to be my Teacher but Jesus. All of these great men and women are lost without Him, all are subject to being spoiled by our devotion to them, and all have an expiration date printed on their lives. *Discipleship requires us to protect our leaders from our excessive love.*

Fifth, there is no sanctuary from scandals. Satan attempts to intrude into every committee or program, and insists on tempting people during even the most solemn moments of life. The reading of Jeremiah 7 brings fear to me and reminds me of my mother's words when I left my business of watchmaking for ministry. "Son," she said seriously, "promise your mother that whenever you sense that your ordination or position or reputation might serve as a smoke screen for bad things in your life—promise me you will return to watchmaking. I would rather see you in heaven as a former watchmaker . . ." and then she remained silent for me to finish her sentence in my mind. *Discipleship means diligently watching over our lives.*

Sixth, tares and wheat must grow together. Jesus will not remove the Judases from His church. That means that church membership is no insurance against hell. Judas lost salvation within a hand's reach of Jesus. What sermons he heard, what miracles he saw, how many conversions he witnessed—who can count? We can be so close, and yet so far! No, the church will not be perfect, cannot be more perfect than I am. Its purity, holiness, efficiency, power we—you and I—increase or decrease. We cannot separate the church's readiness from our own. Our acceptance of His grace and the permission that only we can give to the inner influence of His Spirit are our only hope. He will not hijack people into His kingdom. That is the devil's method.

Discipleship today is a call to get our robes washed and our lamps trimmed. We must learn how to depend on Jesus rather than leaning on people in the church.

Finally, *"everything is politics but politics is not everything,"* argues H. M. Kuitert. Human life is complex, and leading people is the most challenging assignment given to mortals. For example, the consequences of events that happened in the past "conspire" during your tenure as leader, giving you no good option out of the dilemma they create. Someone will be hurt and hurt badly. What politicians will do is not available to us. We cannot lie, cheat, or engage in criminal activity to arrive at a good end. Good ends do not justify evil means. So what do we do? Sin we cannot, hurt we might have to, but only if such a course of action is an exception. Hurting people must not be part of our plans, something we regard as a potential eventual solution to any problems that we might create. Whether by a kiss or by a blow, people must not become instruments in the hands of the powerful. *Discipleship means learning to live God's will God's way.*

CHAPTER 11

The Misplaced Cross

AT THE WRONG TIME AND THE WRONG PLACE

They were twins. Steven had just returned from serving in the military, and Julie, a beautiful, happy young woman, brought hope and help to her aging parents. The two joined the youth of the church and village as they daily worked on the fields of the short-lived communal farms in Yugoslavia. Living on bread, onions, and water, they hoed the cornfields in spring and in the early summer they harvested wheat, corn, sugar beets, hemp, and other produce until the late autumn. The hard work brought just enough income to assure survival during the postwar economic crisis.

That year, in early spring as they worked in a cornfield, one of them hit a bomb with the hoe. The bomb exploded within two feet of them, killing Steven immediately, while Julie bled to death. Some 40 young people watched helplessly as she struggled for about a half hour. No one could help, since no one owned a car, the village had no telephone, and only dirt roads led to the nearest hospital 10 miles away. Shock and fear overwhelmed me, my family, and everyone in the village. What can one say to devastated parents in shock?

Evil is an integral part of human life under Satan's reign. It knows no borders, respects no age, defers to no status, and spares no religious affiliation. Every member of the great human family must face up to it. The Bible recognizes the fact and makes no effort to hide it from us.

Yet it seems that evil inflicts different degrees of pain. Sometimes it comes as a consequence of our own actions. An uncle of mine died from cirrhosis of the liver, a known result of alcoholism. The loss of a dear one for any reason brings us grief, yet when the cause of death is known, it may be easier to deal with. We feel differently if a natural disaster hits, or an unexpected sickness such as cancer strikes close to home. Then a sense of the randomness of evil compounds our pain. We feel even more powerless and carry our cross with more difficulty.

But when we have to suffer because of someone else's foolishness—when in addition to my cross I have to bear a cross that does not belong to me, endure consequences for which I am not responsible—such suffering hurts even more intensely. The additional sense of injustice and capriciousness tests our peace and strains our trust in God. Why should anyone be falsely accused, mistakenly punished, or randomly disabled or killed? How were these two 22-year-old young people connected to Hitler's power fantasies and inhuman cruelty several years after the war? Why did the bomb from his war have to kill them?

On the Friday of Jesus' crucifixion we meet a man who had to cope with similar circumstances. Simon had come to Jerusalem for the Passover feast from the North African town of Cyrene, where a significant Jewish community thrived during the time of Jesus. Until that afternoon Simon had never joined Christ's followers, even though he may have seen and heard Him several times. His sons, Rufus and Alexander, and other acquaintances had told him many wonderful stories about the likely Messiah. As he walks along he notices from afar a crowd leaving the city and knows what such a sight means. The Romans delighted in intimidating their subjects by displaying their cruelty and power during the Jewish feasts. Someone would, no doubt, be tortured and executed on the cross. As he approaches he hears mocking and laughter. Probably he concludes that the people favor the execution of this particular criminal. The mood is different when the Romans lead some patriotic zealot to Calvary. Then people are quiet and the additional troops testify to the Roman fear of revolt. This time, however, only a handful of women cry, and the presence of national leaders gives more credibility to the sentence.

Nevertheless, Simon does not enjoy the sight. Against his better judgment he wanders closer, and then cannot hide his amazement and anger. How can this be? Is this the Jesus of Nazareth? And who has condemned Him to crucifixion? Anger swells in his veins, and the soldiers notice his restlessness. Simon does not know that since the Passover supper Jesus has been betrayed, Judas has committed suicide, Peter has denied any connection with Him, the other disciples have scattered as fast as they could, and Jesus has been completely abandoned. All he knows is that this execution must be a horrible mistake. A short time before, people had shouted "Hosannah" to Him and laid palm branches in His path. Now no one seems to acknowledge Him. Of course, the Romans would immediately crucify anyone who showed the slightest sympathy toward another crucifixion victim, so people had learned to hide their feelings. But still, where were all the sick, blind, lame, devil-possessed, and lepers that Jesus had healed? Had everyone forgotten Him?

Just then Simon feels hands grab him and shove him violently toward Jesus, who lies in the dust, crushed under the weight of the cross. The Gospel of Luke tells it simply: "And as they led him away, they seized one Simon of Cyrene, who was coming in from the country, and laid on him the cross, to carry it behind Jesus" (Luke 23:26).

What has he, Simon, done to deserve this? He's just a passerby minding his own business. The cross on his shoulders is not his own. "Jesus is a nice man, but let me go home," he might have hissed. "He—this Jesus—has been outspoken so many times, but I kept a low profile on purpose. I preoccupied myself with my business and refused to join any party, any group. Religion is all right, but not too much of it. Not if it brings you to this! The times are not favorable for reforms. It's preposterous to think it possible to take on both Roman and Jewish leaders at the same time, as Jesus did."

Angry and revolted at what has happened, Simon slowly follows with the cross, wincing at the cruelty of the barbaric soldiers. But he must not show his feelings, lest the soldiers nail him to a cross also. And as we watch him walk behind Jesus we witness a most unexpected transformation. Simon makes the final decision to be on the side of this Master. He moves from the bleachers into the fight, from being spectator to participant. And in the process he accepts Jesus for what He really is—his Saviour from sin. We find him later as one of the pillars of the church at Antioch, where he preaches to the Gentiles the gospel of Christ (Acts 11:19, 20; 13:1). From Paul's greetings we must conclude that at least part of Simon's family moved to Rome. He writes: "Greet Rufus, eminent in the Lord, also his mother and mine" (Rom. 16:13).

A careful observation of this brief episode during Christ's crucifixion yields several invaluable lessons.

LESSONS OF DISCIPLESHIP

The events of that Friday offer the most cruel of classroom settings. Let's not imagine that Simon considered it a pleasant task to carry the cross for Jesus. At least not in the beginning. No one knew yet what would happen on Sunday. Every step he made under that cross led to the inevitable and final end of all the hopes and dreams many people pinned on Jesus. That Friday the Master became a masterful failure, a public disgrace, especially for those who had followed Him faithfully. The more we realize this, the easier it will be for us to carry our crosses, even the imposed crosses whose outcome we do not yet know.

1. LESSON ABOUT FOLLOWING

It is Friday of the greatest of the feasts in Israel. Sabbath is coming, the greatest Sabbath in the religious experience of his nation. And yet Simon finds himself trapped. He had longed to hear Jesus speak this weekend, to sense the divine presence in His nearness, to receive new assurances that God was still with us. But now the sun crawls across the sky toward the west. If only he could hurry ahead, deposit his disgraceful burden in its spot, and wash his hands and his memory clean of this crime. His family waits for him.

Besides, the Romans are humiliating him on purpose. The people who watch him do this shameful service to the Roman oppressors know that he has no choice in the matter. Surely such a shame happens daily, but why to him, of all people?

Whatever feelings rush through his head, Simon has to concentrate more on what he's doing. A sharp pain from the Roman whip brings him back to reality. He looks around. Jesus is by now unrecognizable. If the abuse continues, someone will have to carry him too to the site of the cross. Around Him the soldiers, like vultures, tear at His flesh without mercy. Some women cry and others moan, adding sound to this tragedy. If only they would be quiet!

Then he spots among the rest of the curious onlookers the proud and mighty leaders, their smiles mingling sadistic pleasure and a sense of impending victory. This Passover feast they will not have to face stiff competition from this Galilean impostor. They, not He, will be the center of attention this time around.

Today, for the first time, Simon can place the actors of this drama in their rightful places. Romans act as Romans, his own people have no power to defend themselves, and the leaders are more despicable than he ever imagined. It is evident that they are behind this outrageous crime, and only because of jealousy and envy. We learn today that because Simon found himself forced to slow down, he had an opportunity to sort out things and people. From this day on he will know where his trust and his loyalty should be.

2. Lesson From Under the Cross

Once he has identified the criminal agents in this tragedy and understood their motives, Simon can focus his attention on Jesus. He remembers the blood-covered, swollen, and disfigured face as he relieved the Master of His burden. Jesus' calm, painful effort to smile at him in gratitude will ever remain in his memory. Any act of kindness, even if coerced, means so much to this exhausted Friend of humanity.

Simon perceives how badly out of place Jesus is here. His pure and noble deportment, His loving and patient reactions contrast sharply with the conduct of His accusers. His self-control and courage to go on, to stumble along the path to His own death, amazes Simon. And right there, under the cross of Jesus, Simon capitulates. This Messiah is not popular, handsome, or charming. He wields no power and promises no prestige or victory. Yet in some strange way He is in greater control of the situation than the soldiers and the priests combined. No insult, no sword, no fatigue, no torture can reach the core of Jesus' being. The Man fascinates Simon.

3. Lesson About Making Disciples

No one and nothing could have previously convinced Simon to pay attention to Jesus. Simon prided himself on being a realist and pragmatist. His sons, Alexander and Rufus (Mark 15:21), probably disciples of Jesus themselves, invited their father many times to find in Him the Saviour and Master. The miracles, the many incredible—even supernatural—signs of His divinity could not tear him loose from his business pursuits.

And when gentle, friendly, and compelling evidences did not reach him, what stronger influence remained? We learn today that God has many agencies at His disposal to give every sincere person a clear opportunity to meet the Saviour. For Moses, He used a burning bush to get his attention. The message came to Balaam through his donkey, and in the case of Naaman, the gentle sweetness of the little slave girl brought her master in contact with his Master. But Simon needed a more irresistible force. The soldiers who ridiculed the Jewish God became His effective instruments. Their very oppression and rudeness kept Simon close enough and long enough with Jesus to reorient his entire course of life for eternity.

4. Lesson About Power

Being a realist, Simon recognizes the injustice, corruption, and ruthless cruelty around him. As he drags the cross he discovers the lesson about power. He himself is innocent of anything that would deserve public disgrace, and he has long believed that undeserved punishment merits a reprisal. As for Jesus, He has done only good (acts of benevolence as no one else could or would do), and He served others for free. So why this senseless and cruel death? Is human life that cheap? Are feelings of jealousy and personal insecurity so important and so powerful that they drive people to kill an innocent man?

Power in human hands, including that of the clergy, is not meant for self-preservation. The only real protection is found in the hands of God and His care. But when power begins to serve personal needs, it becomes a most dangerous tyrant, and no one is safe, including the one who wields it.

5. Lesson About Adversities

Along with Simon we learn that adversities have two faces. The first one we see with our human vision. As we notice the injustices, discrimination, and violence, and feel the pain, our minds and guts churn with the desire for revenge. But when we realize that we really cannot do anything about the situation, we succumb to fear and despair. Evil then appears as an inevitable and invincible overlord.

But Simon experiences the greatest blessing when he looks behind his shame and beyond the cruelty of the moment. He neither searches for nor explores the other face of adversity on purpose. After all, he really has no choice in the matter. The understanding comes to him because Jesus' slow journey to Calvary gives Simon time to think, and because he knows that any thought of revenge is futile. The only thing he can do is stay with Jesus and do for Him whatever He needs the most.

I imagine Simon as very thoughtful and quiet during the holy hours of that Sabbath and for years afterward. At the same time, the newfound joy of seeing his life take deeper meaning, the thrill of being so closely involved in the work of the Messiah, makes him praise God and actually thank Him for Friday's ordeal. As he grasps the meaning of what he has experienced, he begins to understand the love of this Jesus, who, despite shame and disgrace, could control Himself not to wipe them all out in one majestic move of His divine might. That Friday tells him where the real power resides. It teaches him who can really and ultimately protect his soul.

So we learn with Simon that the infamy of bearing imposed crosses need not be the ultimate tragedy. We learn to look for the other face of evil, the one that appears when God becomes involved and when He uses its power to hurt for the purposes of healing, growth, and victory. God can use even evil so that good may come. Only God can do that, and only if we stay with Him closely enough and long enough.

MEANING OF DISCIPLESHIP

Disciples of Jesus, unlike their neighbors, manifest uncommon strength when they face the evils of our earthly existence. No, God does not protect them from its sting. Rather, He enables them to see beyond external appearances the mighty hand that firmly holds their destiny. Simon's affliction sheds light on our trials today.

First, discipleship today requires us to make sure that the formality and routine of Christian life do not hold us back from coming closer to Jesus. What happened in the past when God gave us victories or when He intervenes on our behalf today is not enough to carry us through as future trials strike. Simon had learned how to maintain a nominal form of godliness, one that did not disturb his life or require the courage we need to grow. And our modern search for comfort may urge us to seek that same line of least resistance. We avoid nurturing the mind and cultivating the spirit for the sake of immediate pleasure.

But that is not where the Master seeks to lead us. Rather, He takes us through the training school of trials. In it we develop two important traits. First, we acquire fitness to stand alone and the courage to keep going on. Second, the Master may challenge some disciples to build enough strength to help others by carrying their cross. The apostle Paul put it this way: "Bear one another's burdens, and so fulfil the law of Christ" (Gal. 6:2). *Discipleship today means not only the ability to stand alone, but also to take our brother's or our sister's cross and help them in their adversity.*

Second, in sending us out to announce His coming kingdom, Jesus does not expect us to produce conversions. Our role is only to call, even to urge, people to follow Him. "So we are ambassadors for Christ, God making his appeal through us. We beseech you on behalf of Christ, be reconciled to God" (2 Cor. 5:20). At times we may set goals for baptisms or try to find ways to engage others and thus win them to Him. But after we have done our part in teaching and showing through example who He is, we can rest assured that God has just the right formula to bring them in. (Even unbelieving soldiers can be useful.) He knows the appropriate time and can arrange the right sequence of events. God does not need our gadgets, our brainwashing techniques, our use of fear or intimidation. *Thus, to be a disciple means to be God's instrument through which He can reach His estranged children and woo them back home.*

Third, God calls us today to remember the immense corrupting influence of power—especially if that power is institutionalized, i.e., when constitutions and bylaws give us the right to manipulate other people's destinies and freedoms. It becomes incredibly easy to think of ourselves as irreplaceable, invaluable. We might find ourselves feeling like King Louis XIV of France, who is supposed to have said, *"L'état, c'est moi* ["I am the state"]." In a democracy we may be tempted to think, *I am the majority!* But in Christian context only Jesus' leadership is irreplaceable. So many times we have to remind ourselves that "His work goes forward in spite of us."

True, we might not have any desire to crucify our brother or to kill our sister. But then it may be only because we don't have the prerogatives that Pilate did. It seems to me that the means we use to vent our frustrations, and the intensity of punishment we are likely to impose on others, correspond more to the extent of power that we possess than to the gravity of the wrong committed. The same impulse that prompts a husband to hit his wife may also lead him as a father to abuse his son, as a boss to fire his secretary, as a police officer to beat a suspect to death, as a supreme military commander to declare a war, and as a high priest to execute Jesus.

Hence, *disciples of today heed the words of the Master: "You know that the rulers of the Gentiles lord it over them, and their great men exercise authority over them. It shall not be so among you"* (Matt. 20:25, 26).

Fourth, in the service of the Master assignments constantly vary. Some responsibilities carry more prestige and have more impressive titles. Others might have low pay, no benefits, no health insurance, and no retirement plan. But who is to say that a job is not important if Jesus needs help? If you had a choice to become a high priest (General Conference president) or to help a sentenced criminal carry his cross (provide support to a convict a few hours before execution), what one would you choose? What if you sense that Jesus calls you to be a chaplain rather than an executive? Which is more important?

Think how Simon felt the rest of his life when he remembered that Friday afternoon. He held no high position. In the eyes of onlookers his act could not have been more despicable. Another person held the title of high priest. But whenever we tell the story of Jesus, his name stands far above that of Caiaphas. *Discipleship means lending a hand to the Master when He comes to us as a condemned criminal or a dying AIDS victim. No, Jesus is not totally gone. He did not leave us alone. We still can serve Him by caring for others.*

CHAPTER 12

MYSTERY OF A STOLEN GOD

P ublic opinion concluded that Jesus had failed. Roman power had reestablished the reign of law and order and eliminated another pretender to the Messiahship. The crowds felt confused, the sick and those with disabilities greatly disappointed, the disciples frightened out of their minds, and the leaders jubilant and relieved.

As he leaves Calvary Simon hears people tell their idea of what happened. "Have you seen the priests? What magnificent leadership skills. And they will let nothing stop them to reach their goals. Nothing, I tell you! They have had the last word."

"Jesus? He was a good man. Not a criminal, as they claimed just so they could silence Him. He spoke the truth, He healed the sick, He preached well, but perhaps He was too idealistic. Maybe too naive."

"Yeah, I waited for a miracle. But it was too late. Guess He couldn't handle the situation. Just a Galilean, He was not used to these city-folk tricks. There are no miracles where the Roman boot walks."

"Pilate and the soldiers—man, you should have seen them! I followed the events from the beginning. Pilate had no proof, not for execution. But leadership is leadership. Sometimes you have to choose between two evils."

"I just wonder what His disciples will do. They will have to come out of their holes someday."

"Yes, I know four of them who had a thriving fishing business. Boy, was I glad when they quit. Not for them; glad for me. Less competition, you know."

"And what can they do now?"

"Well, they might come to ask me for a loan to restart. I don't know."

All through the following night the disciples trickle in one by one. The Master had rented the upper room for the duration of the feast. No one speaks much. Peter sits unusually silent. The only thing they all generously share for the rest of the Sabbath is the "fear of the Jews" (John 20:19). Never have Christians been as embarrassed as that Saturday. Why in the world people call it the Great Sabbath I do not understand. Nothing felt or appeared great then. The disciples could not recognize their God, nor could they believe that Jesus had died.

Then comes Sunday. Most of the crowd had already forgotten Jesus, and the disciples had no reason to go out and preach the good news of salvation through Jesus Christ.

But the Gospel of Mark reports three solitary figures leaving Jerusalem early, before the dawn, and heading toward the place where Jesus had been buried (Mark 16:1). In the stillness of the morning you can hear them even as they whisper their thoughts. Their first worry is the stone. "Who will roll away the stone for us from the door of the tomb?" they wonder out loud (verse 3). They want to honor their dead Master by bringing more spices and aromatic oils to anoint His body. The women know they are risking their lives, but it is worth it to them. It was a miracle that the Roman authorities had even allowed them to bury Jesus. Normally they left crucifixion victims up to rot or threw the bodies in a river. Denying a decent burial was the final insult to the victim's family. Even requesting burial for someone crucified could lead to being crucified oneself. And the Romans did not want a victim's grave to become a site of pilgrimage for like-minded conspirators.

Mary of Magdala, one of the women, had many reasons to love Jesus. He had freed her from demons (Luke 8:2), raised her brother Lazarus from the dead (John 11:1-44), and accepted her gratitude when she poured the perfume on His feet (Matt. 26:6-13), so this last gesture of her love is the least she can do in return.

The three women will have a hard task to perform. They hope the soldiers will give them access to the tomb. If any of the men disciples had come along, the Romans might not have granted such a request.

Good thing the soldiers are guarding the body. Tomb robberies have caused much distress, and the women welcome that extra security. No surprises, please. They have faced enough excitement these days.

Try to imagine the shock, the consternation, when, at the bend they see the yawning entrance of the tomb! What? And the soldiers? Those criminals—they've gotten drunk, and now the body is gone. The disciples will be charged with felony, that's what. The body of their Master, which had lain there defenseless, unprotected, has now been stolen.

Suddenly a surge of emotion rushes through her veins, and Mary runs to announce the bad news of the missing Master to the disciples, to the angels, and to Jesus Himself. To the disciples she declares: "They have taken the Lord out of the tomb, and we do not know where they have laid him" (John 20:2). At the question of the angels, "Woman, why are you weeping?" she replies, "Because they have taken away my Lord, and I do not know where they have laid him" (verse 13).

And as she turns away, she notices another man to whom she did not announce the bad news about the stolen body. He asks her, "'Woman, why are you weeping? Whom do you seek?' Supposing him to be the gardener, she said to him, 'Sir, if you have carried him away, tell me where you have laid him, and I will take him away.' Jesus said to her, 'Mary.' She turned and said to him in Hebrew, 'Rab-boni' (which means Teacher). Jesus said to her, 'Do not hold me, for I have not yet ascended to the Father; but go to my brethren and say to them, I am ascending to my Father and your Father, to my God and your God.' Mary Magdalene went and said to the disciples, 'I have seen the Lord'; and she told them that he had said these things to her" (verses 15-18).

LESSONS OF DISCIPLESHIP

The house across the street from us had been vacant for more than a year. Nothing much had happened there, and that's what we'd expected. Whenever a car would stop in its driveway, we'd watch to see if we recognized the real estate agent checking on the property.

Then one day we saw the lights on, heard voices, and noticed cars going in and out. A girl and a boy were playing and running in the yard. We knew then that new neighbors had moved in and taken over the premises.

Life manifests itself. The most devastating death, that of the Life-giver, killed any hope in the hearts of those who believed in Him. Then within a very short time the greatest of miracles produced the most dramatic reversal in human history. In the place where we expected darkness shone light, where we deposited death rose life. We are so excited, tired, and stressed by the traumas and drastic changes of that Passover that only a few major lessons come to mind at this time.

1. LESSON ABOUT MATURE RELIGION

It took great courage to accept the fact that Jesus had actually died. The disciples had had no time yet to answer the question "Now what?" because they had had to attend to the most immediate and urgent stuff—and with as much coolheadedness as possible. They had had to put the feelings of the heart on hold and let simple reason take over. The unbelievable can be true independently of how we feel about it. But by Sunday morning no one among the disciples doubted the reality of the Master's death. It is interesting to notice that no fight erupted when Judas's death produced a vacancy in leadership. No one was first and no one the greatest. Nor did anyone claim to be a hero or trumpet some outstanding achievement. The disciples had not yet recognized Simon of Cyrene as a fellow believer.

So with Jesus suddenly gone, all the relationships became confused. The concept of God as a loving Father, so eloquently taught by Jesus, suffered first. I wonder if anyone prayed that Saturday. How do you pray to God in the name of dead Jesus? How do you love a God who did nothing to protect the best human being from the hands of the worst of us? How do you trust a God who hides His face and abandons His only Son with whom He has declared that He is well pleased? And what chance then do we have—we who cannot come anywhere close to pleasing Him as Jesus did? The whole concept of the supernatural became unpredictable and therefore frightening.

So what lesson did the disciples learn from this desperate situation? Jesus knew what would happen to them and realized that their greatest need would be to develop a direct and mature relationship with God. In fact, He grew increasingly uncomfortable with their codependent and carefree attitude. The disciples now found themselves pushed into the sea of life as Christians to sink or swim. Until then they had not prayed as they needed to, had not focused on the most crucial issues, and had not cared much to establish their own contact with their heavenly Father. Now they had no choice about the matter.

2. LESSON ABOUT BEING THE DISCIPLE OF A DEAD MASTER

Who will teach them now? Whom can they trust? How easy it is to follow if someone walks in front of you, especially if He knows where to go! But like the rest of us they did not fully appreciate the privileges they had had for three and a half years. Think of it—they had had Him listen to them, reason with them, counsel them, and live right before their eyes. All they had needed to do was imitate and succeed.

During that Sabbath, while He rested undisturbed and unreachable, they saw what the world really looked like. Their priorities, values, and goals reversed themselves. And now, because the Master was dead, He could neither shield them from it nor provide a corrective. They would have to learn by searching, asking, praying, and studying God's Word on their own. Each would have to become used to being different without having the Master's authority, popularity, and reputation protect them.

Instead of the dependent life of a student, they had to taste just for those three days a new role. No, they would not continue as before, nor would they all at once become messiahs, totally replacing the Master. Their function would now be to serve as His ambassadors (2 Cor. 5:20) and witnesses (Acts 1:8). They would represent Him and testify of Him to the generations that follow. Paul again caught Christ's intention when he wrote to the churches of Corinth and Philippi: "Be imitators of me, as I am of Christ" (1 Cor. 11:1; cf. Phil. 3:17). It was an entirely new assignment with a heavy weight of responsibility. Life had just begun.

3. LESSONS ABOUT A DEAD GOD

Try to imagine Mary of Magdala's state of mind as an example of the other disciples' thinking. The One she worshiped is dead. Not only can He do nothing; He has to be taken care of, just like the idols of the other nations. Except that they are made of wood and stone, with no danger of smell and contagion. Some of them you could easily fit into your shirt pocket. Mary knows she will have to move His body to anoint it. He cannot hear. You can tell Him whatever nice or rude thing you want, and He will not respond. Mary's God has become a thing, an it.

Now, a religion of an it god is very different from the one Jesus had taught them. The God of heaven is present everywhere, hears everything, and never slumbers, so His emergency help is available for us all the time (Ps. 121:3). Because an it god cannot think, its worshipers have to invent ways to worship it. Its subjects must devise its will. They must guess what pleases it and what they should do to appease it. Mary stood on the threshold of paganism without knowing it. We learn with her how fearful, capricious, and merciless life can be without Christ.

4. LESSON ABOUT A DEAD GOD LIFESTYLE

It may appear at first that a life without God is not only possible, but the very best of lives. You go where you want and do what you want, with no one to obey. I recall a married couple in Canada from my years of pastoring experience there. The woman of the house studied the Bible with me once a week. Her husband always participated in discussions, but they were *her Bible studies*. After dozens of lessons we became good friends. By now I had noticed that the husband was always the one who greeted me, hung my coat in the closet, and ushered me into the living room. Then we waited for his wife to enter. I also became aware of some sort of routine that she performed each time I arrived. First, she would go into her kitchen, put something under her arm, head for the bedroom, and return smiling with her Bible in hand.

One day I asked her husband about her ritual. He looked at me and burst into hilarious laughter. "Oh, Pastor, you are very perceptive. Please—please ask her."

Not knowing what it was all about, I said, "Hey, I do not want to embarrass her. Is it something she's keeping a secret? Why don't you ask her for me?"

"No, Pastor, you ask. I guarantee you it's OK."

So I did. The woman blushed a bit, sighed, and said, "Well, Pastor, come and see."

I followed her to her kitchen. There on the wall she showed me an empty shrine. "What do you normally keep there?" I asked.

"A saint," she said, mentioning her name. "You see, Pastor, when you come here with the Bible, I know we will be finding all sorts of things in it that would not please my saint. So I take her into my bedroom, close the door so she cannot hear us, and when you're gone I bring her back to her place in the kitchen."

Think of it. You know a god forbids stealing, so you just hide him, and he cannot know what you're doing. He teaches that lying, cheating, or gossiping is bad, so you do it just when you're on vacation and everything is fine. Turn your back to your god, and evil becomes neutral or even good. Hide him or cover him up, and there is your freedom to act as you please.

With Mary we learn that there is no other god except the God of heaven. Without Him the cosmos becomes chaos. Every aspect of human life turns into disaster. But a dead Jesus during that Sabbath day does not mean a dead God. No matter how much we may become used to Him, we cannot reduce the true God to an it. In the episode that follows, this very lesson became vivid to Mary for the rest of her life.

5. Lesson From a Gardener

Whereas Mary had expected a sealed tomb, the cave now yawned open. Although she had wanted darkness, there was light, and where she had anticipated finding a corpse, she encountered an empty tomb with folded linen. Instantly she concluded that some-one had taken Him away. Her God was stolen.

Then something happened when the "gardener" spoke. Everything changed in one majestic instant. Her life, her universe, turned right side up! The chaos she stared at turned into a magnifi-cent cosmos before her very eyes. She did not think much of "gar-deners" before. But this would teach her!

The "gardener" became Jesus when she heard her name. A sim-ple "Mary" transformed her life. Jesus addressed her directly, person-ally, and the it became the He. An impersonal religion became a per-sonal relationship, and a dead God became the Life-giver again. She could neither hide Him nor hide from Him. Her life was wide open before Him, allowing Him to mold her, to protect her, and to give her existence meaning.

Like a volcano, Mary erupts into a messenger of good news. She bursts into the room where disciples stretch and yawn and shouts exuberantly: "I have seen the Lord" (John 20:18).

6. "Hands Off!"

And, as her world changes, so her relationship to Jesus must. I imagine her wanting to give Him a hug. A good old bear hug. But Jesus says firmly, "Do not hold me" (verse 17), or as other versions legitimately translate: "Touch me not" (KJV) or "Do not cling to me" (NEB), or "Touch me no more" (NEB, margin).

Jesus is a dead corpse no longer, so you cannot handle and move Him at will; He is not an idol that you can hide from; nor is He a gardener whom you could accuse of stealing His body. "Hello, Mary, but I must first get in touch with My Father. You remember, on Friday I could not see His face. Now I must gaze at it. I am very glad to see you, Mary, but My Father is first. I have an appointment—a most vital appointment. I want first to see Him, to hear Him tell Me that the bridge that I have come to be for you sinners can indeed reach all the way to the other side. I must see Him first."

As a victor over sin and death, Jesus assumes His position as her Lord and Saviour. No, He does not need spices or anointing to pre-serve Him from the corruption of death. He has life in Himself and can be God by Himself.

Now Mary can look at the same stone, the same empty tomb, the angels, and her "Gardener," and she would rather do nothing to "improve" the situation. The lesson? Yes, Jesus is our friend, teacher, and brother. He forgives our sins, washes our feet, and overlooks our childish ways. But He is God and a Lord who abides in an unapproachable light (1 Tim. 6:16), where He longs to hide us from the forces of evil.

MEANING OF DISCIPLESHIP

We find great wealth of meaning in this dramatic lesson. From the pit of death Jesus ushers us into an eternal life of victories. The events that follow the resurrection of Jesus form a deliberate process of graduating disciples from studies to service, from learning with Jesus to working with Him. This is where you and I fit as well.

First, there is a fact—a very meaningful truth—that we must face today: our God is not dead. This is why our neighbors can see His light in our eyes, or hear His voice from our mouth. Even though we may have been Christians for long decades, with two, three, or four generations of discipleship behind us, can we still distinguish between our opinions and His will? We are careful that our knowledge, our experience, our blessings, and a rich harvest of fruits in His work do not push God behind, as if He were an it, a thing we can bypass or ignore. *Discipleship today means to resist the temptation to act independently or to modify His will for us so it fits our fancy, just because He is not physically present among us to intervene immediately.*

Second, Jesus would like to give us sufficient autonomy to shape His program according to our personality. While His will remains sovereign, our individual gifts can be formatted so they will appeal to the contemporary culture and bring it to higher levels of moral excellence. *Discipleship challenges us to remain true to God's intent and at the same time be relevant and attractive to the age we minister to.*

Third, it is not true that evangelistic fervor has vanished from His church. Just look how people sell Avon or any other product when they are convinced of its effectiveness. Consider Mary. She did not need all the workshops and all the helps and all the computerized support to face disciples, angels, and Jesus Himself, telling them what she believed to be the truth. *Discipleship today calls us to examine our commitment and measure the depth of our conviction that Christianity is truly the best "product" on the market today. I sense that this kind of reality check may be a key to revival and outreach.*

Fourth, we have a choice today as to who will lead us. The god from whom we can hide is a most accommodating lord. He will not impose his will, he will close his eyes when we hurt ourselves, and he can be manipulated, outvoted, politicized, sold, and traded in at will. The problem with this kind of "church discipline," "caring," or "freedom" is that the same manipulations and customizing will be considered legitimate even when someone does injustice to us. The god from whom we can hide is the same god from whom our enemies and criminals can hide as well, so they can hurt us with impunity. *Discipleship today calls us to reject cheap religiosity, emotionalism, and the plain naïveté that God cannot hear or see. It summons us to fall at the feet of our "gardener" and exclaim with Thomas, "My Lord and my God!" (John 20:28).*

Fifth, we would do well to remember that we do not own Jesus. No religious denomination, no nationality, and no social class has a monopoly on Him. The risen Master is saying:

● "Hands off" to all of us who think that God cannot be God without our well-intended spices, our money, our degrees, or our talents.

● "Hands off" to me if I think that I can hide God behind my back so that I can do what I please.

● "Hands off" to those who in His name and the name of national religion claim the right to exterminate the "others" until only like-minded people remain in our neighborhoods.

● "Hands off" to me if I think that Jesus can be stolen and that I can keep watch over Him and assume the right to decide who can approach Him.

● "Hands off" to those of us who dare steal money from His purse and flirt with our brother's wife just because He is not physically present.

He is alive and knows our suffering. Having saved all our tears (see Ps. 56:8), He never forgets or hushes up injustice and pain. God is never unmindful of our rights.

Sixth, the wonderful news that the tomb is open and that the "gardener" is our living Lord and Saviour; He can make us lift our heads and voices in the song of victory. We are not left prey to the evil one. For a "weekend" it might seem that at Auschwitz or Vukovar or Golgotha that our God is dead. Or that He is shut up in some closet or that in His apartment there is no light and that the "gardeners" call the shots. But on that morning the Roman might fell to the dust and the angel removed the stone of human control over divinity. Then, quietly, the angels watched as Jesus folded His linen neatly and came out holding in His hands the final victory that is yours and mine.

AFTERWORD

"He will feed his flock like a shepherd, he will gather the lambs in his arms, he will carry them in his bosom, and gently lead those that are with young" (Isa. 40:11).

This is the experience of the ages. An experience fulfilled for millennia. Christ has never left any one of His flock to their own devices if they have chosen to follow Him. God plans for every emergency and every need. Those young in faith or young in age did not have to worry about the rough road ahead and the weakness of their resources. He gathered them and carried them in His bosom. The older ones, those who carry the burdens of duty or the weight of age, He led slowly. His church has been moving because He does. It did not stagnate as some wished, nor did it race ahead as others tried to push it.

"The Lord is my shepherd, I shall not want. . . ."

This is the present reality. Disciples do not always know what to expect, but that is all right, because they follow the One who calms the storms, heals the sick, feeds the hungry, raises the dead, and defeats the devil. Nothing can challenge Him. We may be hungry, but He satisfies our need. When we are thirsty, He leads us to still waters, and our cup of blessings is full. While those who follow Jesus pass through the valley of the shadow of death, they do not stay there. Jesus has overcome the power of the tomb forever.

Revelation 14:4, 5 presents to us the future reality of those who follow the Lamb wherever He goes. They will sing the song of battle and victory, of trial and success, of sickness and healing, of failure and success, and of death and resurrection. As disciples they keep themselves so close to the Master that sin and evil cannot cling to them. And as a result, "in their mouth no lie [is] found, for they are spotless" (verse 5).

Today He walks by your place. You can see Him veering from His path just for your sake. Then, looking you in the eyes, He calls, "Follow Me."